Quitting Church

Quitting Church

WHY THE FAITHFUL ARE FLEEING AND WHAT TO DO ABOUT IT

JULIA DUIN

BakerBooks
a division of Baker Publishing Group
Grand Rapids, Michigan

© 2008 by Julia Duin

Published by Baker Books
a division of Baker Publishing Group
P.O. Box 6287, Grand Rapids, MI 49516-6287
www.bakerbooks.com

Printed in the United States of America

Library of Congress Cataloging-in-Publication Data
Duin, Julia.
    Quitting church : why the faithful are fleeing and what to do about it / Julia
Duin.
        p.   cm.
    Includes bibliographical references.
    ISBN 978-0-8010-6823-2 (cloth)
    1. Church attendance. 2. Church membership. I. Title.
BV652.5.D85 2008
277.3′083—dc22   2008020161

Scripture is taken from the King James Version of the Bible.

Materials from several chapters appeared previously in online essays posted at www
.BreakPoint.org, copyright Prison Fellowship, 2007. Used with permission.

To Rebecca and Sue,
Pam and Dick,
Linda, Karen and Wilt,
and the many other believers who long
for a decent church.

CONTENTS

1. The Flood Outward 9
   Why So Many Good People Are Leaving

2. The Irrelevant Church 27
   Give Them a Reason to Be Here

3. Searching for Community 47
   What We Really Wish Church Could Be

4. Emergence and Resurgence 67
   Adjusting to the Twenty-first Century

5. The Loneliest Number 83
   Why Singles over Thirty-five Are Saying Good-bye

6. Not So Solid Teaching 101
   Why Christians Cannot Exit the Obstetrics Ward

7. Is the Pastor the Problem? 117
   Or Is the Whole System Broken?

8. The Other Sex 135
   Why Many Women Are Fed Up

9. Bewildered Charismatics   151
   Looking for the Spirit in a Parched Land

10. Bringing Them Back   169
    If They Want to Come

   Sources   181

1

~~~~~~~~~~

THE FLOOD OUTWARD

Why So Many Good People Are Leaving

"You're not going to church?" I asked him.

It was his birthday, so we had met for dinner at the Olive Garden, one of our favorite Italian restaurants. He shook his head. "Matt," I will call him, was legally blind and unable to drive. That and a few other handicaps had not prevented him from having a decent-paying job with the U.S. government, from amassing a world-class library in his home, and from being the go-to guy with answers to all my questions about Reformed theology.

But here he was, disconsolate. A reporter by trade, I dragged his story out of him.

"I don't mind taking the metro to church, but you know me," he said, "I'm pretty Reformed, and the kind of church I like is always at least two miles from the nearest stop."

~~~~~~~~~~

I named a church in Alexandria, a posh suburb with its own historic district. He'd been going there the last time we talked.

"Oh, they promised they'd find me a family that could pick me up," he said. "And they did, for a while. Then they started forgetting I was there. It was like Russian roulette. I would get dressed and wait for them, but I never knew which Sunday they'd actually show up at my front door."

By the time he'd get this family on their cell phone, they'd already be in the church parking lot and in no mood to double back and get him. When he brought this up to the leaders at his church, they told him he was on his own. Finally he just quit going for more than a year. No one from his church ever called to ask where he was. He contacted some other churches, but none would offer him any help in getting to their services.

I was stunned. If anyone was in love with God, it was Matt. He was single and male, rare in church these days. But no one wanted him. In fact no one wanted a bunch of my friends. There was Gwen in Salem, Oregon, whose pastor would never say more than a few words to her. Struggling to bring up three kids alone, she could have used his moral support. "But pastors don't pal around with single moms," she told me. "Too many needs and we're not big enough givers." She finally dropped out of her Pentecostal congregation.

Then there were Paul and Ed, two journalist friends in Richmond, Virginia, and Casper, Wyoming. Both brilliant evangelical men, they told me they loved the Lord but couldn't live with the paucity of spiritual maturity in every congregation they visited. Both were now church dropouts.

And there was Maeve, a married friend whose husband had talked back to the elders at their former congregation, a large Bible church also in northern Virginia. The elders kicked them both out. This couple found some refuge in a smaller, evangelical congregation, but, "I go only out of obedience," she told me over lunch one day.

She was referring to the admonition in Hebrews 10:25 against "forsaking the assembling of ourselves together," a verse commonly used to exhort one's friends not to skip out on other Christians and, by extension, the Lord. The verse is framed with commands to "consider one another to provoke unto love and to good works" and that Christians should be "exhorting one another."

Those commands weren't put to use with people like her.

"The church is not like Christ," she added sadly.

Slipping Out

Those are just my personal friends. As for people I interview in my day-to-day job as a religion reporter, I was discovering that many, many evangelical Christians are slipping out or barely hanging on to their churches. It's no secret that the percentage of Americans in church on any given Sunday is dropping fast. Religious attendance fell from 41 percent in 1971 to 31 percent in 2002, according to a survey sponsored by the National Opinion Research Center at the University of Chicago. For years, Gallup polls have shown American church attendance hovering at 43 percent of the population, which would mean 129 million out of an estimated 300 million Americans at the end of 2006. However, two 2005 studies, one by sociologists C. Kirk Hadaway and Penny Long Marler and the other by Dave Olson, a researcher for the Evangelical Covenant Church, show that a more accurate attendance percentage is in the 18th to 20th percentile, half of what Gallup shows.

A significantly smaller number of Americans "are participating in the most basic Christian practices: the weekly gathering for worship, teaching, prayer and fellowship," Olson said in the April 2006 issue of *Christianity Today*.

Hadaway and Marler faulted the complexities of American life—exhaustion, traffic, two working parents, even children's soccer games increasingly getting scheduled on Sundays—as the main reason people give themselves much more leniency in skipping church. They have a point, but I remember thirty years ago when America was in the middle of the Jesus Movement. Back then no one dared miss all the amazing things going on during a Sunday morning service.

How things have changed!

The three fastest-growing church groups, according to the *2007 Yearbook of American and Canadian Churches*, were Assemblies of God, Mormons, and Catholics. The Southern Baptists, long a growing denomination, saw its baptisms *drop* at the midpoint of the decade. A lot of growth in the Catholic Church was due to immigrants. One-third of immigrants switch to Protestant churches within a generation, according to Edwin Hernandez, a research fellow for the Center for the Study of Latino Religion at the University of Notre Dame. However, not all those departing Catholics are ending up in Protestant churches. Because evangelicals were for a long time the political flavor of the month due to a two-term Bush presidency, most secular pundits paint church members as a large, powerful monolith that moves in time to commands from Focus on the Family and can mobilize millions of voters to act through the words of a few spokesmen. This is hugely inaccurate. It's true that evangelicals can work powerfully in concert, but their numbers are not growing appreciably. Much church growth is due to transfers from one church to another.

None of this is to say spiritually interested people are not out there. The packed churches nationwide after September 11 show they are. We all know how the terrorist attacks provoked a growth spurt in church attendance, only to have it die down within a month after the seekers melted away, unimpressed.

Because the U.S. population is expanding, evangelical pollster George Barna estimates the number of unchurched Americans is growing by about one million each year. The fraction of Americans with no religious preference doubled during the 1990s from 8 to 14 percent, according to a 2001 City University of New York "American Religious Identification Survey." However, of that 14 percent, less than half (40 percent) were atheists; the other 60 percent were merely "religious" or "spiritual." In other words, plenty of people in this country are interested in spiritual matters. They are simply not going to church to feed this interest.

Why? I have sensed for several years something is not right with church life, especially with evangelical church life. It's been reported many times that most Americans have fled mainline Protestant churches in the past half century, cutting denominations such as the Episcopal Church and Presbyterian Church USA by half. But in the past decade, it's the evangelical churches that are losing ground.

These are not the large megachurches on which all the media are fixated. Ten percent of America's 331,000 congregations have more than 350 members, but more than half of those attending religious services go to those 33,000 or so churches, according to the University of Arizona's 1998 National Congregations Study. Or, as the study said, although most churches are small, most people are in large churches. For instance, 28 percent of all churchgoers are Roman Catholic, but only 6 percent of all congregations are

Catholic. Catholic congregations have always been huge, partly due to the shortage of priests. Their large, often impersonal nature—one priest to every 3,640 Catholics—makes it easy for smaller Protestant congregations to pick them off.

Yet not all Protestant churches are doing well. Seventy-one percent of all congregations, said the Arizona study, have fewer than one hundred participating adults. *A Field Guide to U.S. Congregations*, published in 2002 by Cynthia Woolever and Deborah Bruce, put it this way: America is like a hypothetical town of one thousand, divided among ten congregations. Eight of the ten would be small and more than half of the people would worship in two large churches, one of them being Roman Catholic.

It's an odd pattern. Americans like small groups but prefer big churches. And in recent years, they've found more and more churches, big and small, that aren't relevant to their lives. I was born again in the Pacific Northwest during the Jesus Movement, so I was used to burgeoning churches in Seattle during my teens. When my parents moved to the Washington, D.C., area, I spent my college summers there. At the time, the metro Washington area was bursting with lively evangelical, charismatic, even messianic Jewish congregations. Christian radio stations and Jesus music festivals were hot. The Catholic charismatic prayer meetings all over the DC area were powerful and evangelistic. Every Tuesday night, some two thousand college-aged people packed into Christ Church on Massachusetts Avenue for a powerful evangelical Protestant service called TAG (for "Take and Give"), filled with powerful preaching by men not much older than I. During the service, amazing prophecies were given. Converts poured out of that place by the hundreds.

The 1980s

Returning to Portland for my first newspaper job, I began to notice how the best congregations suffered bizarre splits, how often pastors got trapped into horrendous sexual situations, and how much of the fallout landed on the members. One of my reporting specialties was Christian communities, having lived in a radical one in downtown Portland—we pooled salaries even—during the community heyday in the 1970s. Yet by 1990 nearly every Christian community in the country had dissolved or dramatically shrunk in numbers.

Lots of folks ended up in regular churches, their once radical Christian lives domesticated and tranquilized. By the late 1980s, I was a religion reporter for the *Houston Chronicle*, spending much of my time covering the televangelist scandals that followed one after another in 1987 and 1988. Although Pat Robertson's run for the presidency in 1988 bespoke a new evangelical political power, the spiritual power so evident in churches I attended in the 1970s had evaporated. Church growth techniques were substituted. Everyone was into inner healing.

Meanwhile, books like Phil Yancey's 1988 book *Disappointment with God* and Ron Enroth's 1992 *Churches That Abuse* (which he followed up with a sequel in 1994) were coming out, hinting at a darker reality undergirding American "churchdom."

In 1990 I began writing a history of Houston's Episcopal Church of the Redeemer, for years a bright light in the worldwide charismatic renewal. Its pastor, Graham Pulkingham, was a major founder of the movement, and the flood of music that poured out of that church still echoes in many congregations today. As I traveled the country interviewing former members, I was amazed to find, over and over, people who had dropped out of church. The most common theme was the banality of the local church, especially after having experienced so much supernatural power in Houston. Redeemer, people told me, ruined you for life at any other church. There they had experienced fabulous worship, great preaching, spiritual gifts, and sacrificial giving so that newcomers were converted almost as soon as they walked into the place. Once they left Houston, it was hard to find anything close.

These people were experienced believers. Many had joined other churches, then slowly dropped out, when either a pastor saw them as a threat or the spiritual gruel offered Sunday after Sunday just became unpalatable. At the time, I wrote off a lot of these people as just not trying hard enough to find a good church. After all, when I had left Houston to attend seminary near Pittsburgh, I had found several good churches.

However, my next move, to northwestern New Mexico in 1994, helped me to understand their frustration. The local Episcopal Church was twenty years behind the vibrant churches I was used to. I taught Sunday school there but was unable to make friends. Finally I fled to an Assemblies of God congregation and chalked up my church-hunting difficulties to the isolated corner of the state I lived in.

But my next move, to Virginia, turned up worse problems in finding a church. The Washington region, a spiritual powerhouse in the 1970s, had shifted dramatically twenty-five years later. Once spiritually powerful churches had become "seeker-friendly" congregations, and their main aim seemed to be to make the service as short as possible. Everything seemed packaged. TAG had morphed into a megachurch that had dropped its freewheeling charismatic distinctives for a much more staid service that emphasized writings by Charles Spurgeon and other Reformed theologians. The bookstore was stocked only with books personally approved by the pastor.

The once vibrant Catholic charismatic prayer meetings in the area had vanished, except for one very quiet group meeting in a Maryland suburb. There were a number of large Protestant congregations, but most revolved around the personality of their pastor. A 1994 Canadian revival known as the "Toronto blessing" livened up some church services for a few years, but by 1997 the biggest spiritual event going was the Promise Keepers meeting on the Mall. And within two years of that, the national men's group was scraping for funds and downsizing. And then a promising revival in Pensacola, Florida, degenerated into splits among its leaders. Dryness was everywhere.

No Watering Hole

I was having breakfast in a trendy restaurant in the northern Virginia suburb of Arlington when I broached the subject with two friends. They too knew of many people who were desperate to find spiritual food and drink from their churches. "But there's very little out there of substance," one friend said. "All these thirsty people and no watering hole." What a poignant commentary on the current landscape of American Christianity!

And the problem wasn't just local. Many of my favorite church haunts from Portland in the 1970s were on the ropes. I heard from friends living near Los Angeles about how all the congregations they encountered were just reinventing the wheel. One Sunday during a business trip to Ft. Lauderdale, I dropped by what is supposedly the largest church in the county. I found a windowless sanctuary where all the activity was centered on the stage, while the audience—we were not truly a congregation, it seemed—sat passively for two hours. The only time the people there looked alive was after the service at the church's fabulous organic cafeteria.

A lot of evangelical leaders do not see a problem. In the late 1990s a group of journalists had a conference phone call with several such Christian leaders. One was the late Bill Bright, founder of Campus Crusade. He insisted America was on the threshold of national revival because he saw the growth of a vibrant prayer movement on his speaking tours. Several of us challenged him, saying we remembered all too well how much livelier American religion was in the seventies. Where was his proof that things were better now? He could not say.

In early 2006 I emailed the local head of a national evangelistic campus Christian ministry, asking if he saw much going on spiritually in his circles. "I just don't see signs of revival at all," he said. "In fact just the opposite. I see a lot of shallow evangelicals who are tossed to and fro by the culture." Things were better, we both agreed, in the days when we were in college. "The current situation speaks loudly about how evangelical campus groups understand their priorities for being on campus these days," he told me. "It's fellowship, not evangelism, that is most groups' reason for existence, which is sad."

If campuses, which are usually the cutting edge of trends, are showing major slippage, I wonder where else the exodus is showing up. Are these examples like the canary in the mine, showing that spiritual oxygen is running out?

The problem seems to be the church itself. Survey after survey says many Americans continue their private religious practices, such as reading the Bible, praying to God, and even sharing their faith in Jesus Christ. But they have given up on the institution. I kept encountering people who had been converted back in the Jesus Movement days of the 1970s. Many said they were too disheartened to attend church now, knowing how vibrant it used to be and how dead it seems now.

Then I found an essay, posted on a Listserv by revival historian Andrew Strom, about a similar "out of church" phenomenon in New Zealand. The people opting out of church had been leaders, the most committed, but as the years wore on, they simply could not stand to sit and "watch the same old game being played anymore," he said. "The lack of God is what gets to them, even in our most 'Spirit-filled' churches."

He continued, "New fads and programs come and go, but mediocrity and lack of God just seem to go on forever. And so quietly, sometimes without anyone even noticing, they slowly slip out the doors, never to return."

So it's not just us Americans, I thought. After he posted this essay, he got reams of emails, he said, "which confirmed to me that this issue is so much larger than many of us have realized. I don't think a lot of Christian leaders have any clue how many believers are simply opting out of organized religion today."

A short time later, in quick succession, I noticed articles in *Charisma* and *Christianity Today* about Christians opting out of church. It was amazing to read some of the letters to the editor in these magazines. "Do you want to know why Christians are leaving the 'bricks and mortar church'?" one person asked in *Charisma's* April 2005 letters-to-the-editor section. "Could it be that the church is dysfunctional and does not know its true role in the lives of believers?" A letter to the editor in the March 2006 *Christianity Today* said today's church dropout is not interested in a "weakened local church. Instead we are seeking a departure from a

Christian subculture that has developed over the last twenty years, and a return to a faith that is authentic, relevant, and applicable.

"In our minds, the local church has become its own culture—from megachurches with creative marketing campaigns to Christian music, Christian books, Christian clothing, and even Christian weight-loss programs. These things, in and of themselves, are well and good—but they are no substitute for a fleshed-out faith."

Others talked about legalism, turf battles, and worship that had become entertainment. None of these writers wanted to quit church; they felt pushed out or that leaving was taking the high road. "Many of us dropouts tried to work behind the scenes to keep unity," one wrote to *Charisma*. "But if we spoke out, we were 'in rebellion.' Many of us chose to leave rather than start wars."

Furthermore, no army can fight if huge numbers of its members have gone AWOL. Hadaway and Marler estimated as much as 78 million Protestants belong to this camp of no-shows. That sounds high to me, but still, why have many of the church's best soldiers laid down their arms in disgust?

Bailing Out

In the fall of 2005 a new book landed on my desk: *Why Men Hate Going to Church* by David Murrow. It showed a sleeping man draped over a pew. The book reported that men are not walking out of church, they're running out.

Then I had an interview with George Barna about his new book, *Revolution*, in which he mourns the multitudes running out the door. Not only have the men bailed out, he said, many of the women are following them.

In the first days of 2006, *Charisma* printed a message by evangelist Steve Hill (one of several men behind the mid-1990s revival at an Assembly of God church in Pensacola), who called much of what's happening in today's churches "eye candy."

And in the January issue of *Discipleship Journal*, one of the lead stories was "How to Survive Church: Hope for Disillusioned Churchgoers."

In March *Time* magazine announced "some evangelicals are abandoning megachurches for minichurches—based in their own living rooms." It was about the growth of house churches among disgruntled American evangelicals. We used to joke at my newspaper that by the time a news magazine got around to reporting a trend, it was always old news, especially when it concerned religion. So if *Time* had already tracked this trend, obviously the exodus was in full swing.

So it's official: evangelicals, for a variety of reasons, are heading out of church—not all of them and not everywhere, but the trend is undeniable. Sunday mornings at church have become too banal, boring, or painful. Large groups of Christians are opting out of church because they find it impossible to stay.

In 2002 Barna gave *Christianity Today* "nine challenges" for American Christians.

1. Worship is stale: the "same old same old."
2. Evangelicals are watering down their theological beliefs.
3. Evangelical congregations are still by and large split into all-white, all-black, or all-Hispanic groups. That shouldn't be.
4. Many Christians, especially younger ones, don't take the Bible seriously, especially on issues such as divorce and premarital sex.

5. Christianity in America has essentially no built-in cost.
6. Any expression of the supernatural has been excised from Sunday worship.
7. No one is ready for the fact that Gen Y Christians are going to radically reinvent the church.
8. U.S. churches tend to compete rather than cooperate.
9. There is a dearth of good leaders. Those who fill America's pulpits, he said, are teachers—good people all—but not leaders with a vision.

After reading that, I began to wonder if the evangelical monolith is simply the emperor before losing his clothes. The form is there, but the substance—the strength and the people—has long departed.

My research fleshed out Barna's data. Also I ran across something impossible to measure in a survey: many people I encountered were disappointed or perplexed in some way with God. They'd been Christians for more than a decade, and some had experienced serious suffering. The more honest ones admitted something was not working in their Christian faith. They were not connecting with God as to the reason for their sorrows; in fact God seemed to be confounding their prayers. Their churches were useless in giving meaningful counsel, and if these people brought up their concerns in a Bible study, their doubts and anger toward God were frowned on by others in the group. They were like wounded soldiers returning from Iraq and Afghanistan to a country that barely knew they were at war. Such people needed sermons on unanswered prayer, but their pastors were giving PowerPoint presentations on attaining breakthroughs.

My research suggested that people are simply not being pastored. Often ministers are out of touch with what's happening on the ground, as they are surrounded by a wall of secretaries and voice mail. Congregants have to wait up to a month for an appointment, if they can get in at all. Once-a-week home Bible study groups lack depth and theological know-how for help with the serious problems many of us face. Many churches refer people to professional counseling that costs at least seventy-five dollars an hour. Those lucky enough to have a health plan that pays for counseling usually find the only counselors on approved HMO lists have no concept of a Christian worldview.

I ran into demographic groups, such as men and singles, who have abandoned the church in large numbers because they are fed up with their needs never being addressed. Singles are the largest demographic among the unchurched. A third group, working moms, is about to join those two demographics. Many people are no longer content to waste part of their Sundays on an institution that gives them nothing.

Other concerns that alienate people are church scandals, irrelevancy, an inefficient leadership model, the quenching of supernatural spiritual gifts during Sunday worship, clergy who are too controlling of passive congregations, the impersonal nature of the typical service—and the list goes on.

This book is an attempt to get at the roots of these problems, understand why people are bailing out, and offer some ideas—my own and those of others—on what would bring them back. The hour is not too late. But if nothing is done, this exodus of desperation, this boycott, will continue.

Lastly, although this is a fascinating phenomenon from a sociological viewpoint, it is also intensely personal. I have two brothers who, like me, are born-again Christians. When I began researching this book, none of us belonged to a church. Disheartened, we had all dropped out of congregations near Portland, Seattle, and northern Virginia. I was part of a large exodus from a church that lost half its members—about four hundred people—in just a few years.

I pulled out in 2001. I would be churchless for the next six years. That's not something I had planned. My desk has several books piled on it describing the sad state of the church, written by journalists who were once evangelical but who are no longer or who have abandoned their faith. Theirs was not a road I wanted to take.

Back in 1998 I was discussing my situation with some friends in Winthrop, just over the Cascade Mountains in the eastern part of Washington State. It was a sunny May afternoon, and we were walking through a meadow covered with purple lupine, larkspur, sunflowers, mustard, balsamroot, pink bitterroot—a zoo of flowers. I was describing my church as we looked out on the north Cascades.

"Oh, you'll leave," they said, "because they won't change. Either you change or you leave."

Not me, I said. I had always criticized those who had left church. But within three years, I was gone. For the first time in almost thirty years of attending evangelical churches, I was throwing in the towel. Like my friend Matt at the Olive Garden, I gave up. And I was surprised to find how little I missed going to church; it was a relief to avoid the bizarre treatment I had gotten from leaders there. I did stick with a Wednesday night home group, which fulfilled many of the functions of a church, for five years. Then that group dissolved by mutual consent in January 2006. A month later a Christian journalists fellowship I'd been part of fell apart unexpectedly. Other than a friend who was a weekly prayer partner, I was truly going it alone.

Eventually I did end up back in a church, but on the road to arriving there, I began asking questions and structuring people's responses in several categories as to why the faithful are fleeing. It's not hard to find the reason so many are heading out the door; the trick is how to stir back to life what remains.

2

◇◇◇◇◇◇◇◇

THE IRRELEVANT CHURCH

Give Them a Reason to Be Here

During the summer of 2007, an amazing essay was splashed across the front page of the *Los Angeles Times*. The writer, Bill Lobdell, was the paper's former religion writer and known as a born-again Christian by several of us working in the same field. After hitting a home run in 2004 with his exposé on the luxurious lifestyles of the founders of Trinity Broadcasting Network in Orange County, he inexplicably disappeared from the beat. Later he surfaced at the *Times* Orange County bureau.

His essay traced a fifteen-year path that started with his conversion in his twenties at a retreat, and later his assignment to the religion beat, where his first three years were a glorious succession of fabulously interesting stories. Then came the Catholic abuse scandal of 2002. Lobdell, who was considering becoming a Catholic, wrote about the corruption he saw firsthand among priests and bishops and how, for the most part, parishioners went along with it. He also detailed his disgust with a Benny Hinn crusade where the sick were not getting healed. As the years went on, no matter where he turned, he found corruption.

Worst of all, no one was talking about it. No one was preaching about the sexual abuses from the Catholic pulpits, and there were very few personalities in the evangelical Protestant world who were addressing the excesses of prosperity theology. Something had to go, and it was Lobdell's faith.

"For some time, I had tried to push away doubts and reconcile an all-powerful and infinitely loving God with what I saw, but I was losing ground," he wrote. "I wondered if my born-again experience at the mountain retreat was more about fatigue, spiritual longing, and emotional vulnerability than being touched by Jesus. And I considered another possibility: Maybe God didn't exist."

The piece struck a nerve, judging from the two thousand emails Lobdell got in response to his essay (typically, fifty emails are considered a big response for the average news story). Most of the responses were sympathetic to his crisis of faith. Quite a few religion bloggers took the topic on. One of the best discussions was on Rod Dreher's Crunchycon blog on Beliefnet.com. Several bloggers criticized Lobdell for simply failing to find the right church, then taking out his angst on the general public.

"I don't know the guy," Dreher responded, "but his piece doesn't read like he was looking for the perfect church. What he saw was evil in the leadership of various churches, and a laity that accepted, and even promoted it. He quit being able to believe. It's not that he mourns the loss of a perfect church. This is much deeper, it seems to me."

Lobdell's piece did a fabulous job of illustrating one of the chief reasons people leave church. What's preached and taught is irrelevant to the questions on the ground. Catholics in particular see a disconnect between what's coming from the pulpit and people's real lives, says Judie Brown, president of the American Life League (ALL), a pro-life group in Stafford, Virginia. In the spring of 2007, her newest book, *Saving Those Damned Catholics*, landed on my desk at work. It was dedicated to a woman named Geraldine, Judie's best friend.

"She became so distraught at the pablum-puking sermons she was hearing, she decided not to go to Mass anymore," Brown told me. "She was shopping for parishes in the area of the Diocese of Orange [California], and not finding anything."

Three months after Geraldine left church, she died of congestive heart failure. Brown was haunted by her friend's despair.

"This is so prevalent in the church today," she told me. "There is so much to be discouraged about and little to rejoice about unless you have a great priest, like I do. But most Catholics hear in a sermon about either the death penalty or something from the comics in the newspapers. The homilies are irrelevant to their daily lives."

They're also irrelevant to church teaching, she added. "Catholics know what the church teaches on contraception, they ask the pastor why he is not preaching on it, and he says, 'I don't want to lose financial support.' That sickens them," she said. "One reason why 85 percent of Catholics support contraception is they have not been catechized correctly. They do not know about natural family planning; they do not know why contraception is evil." (Catholic teaching mandates that all sexual intercourse must have the potential of creating life; therefore, artificial birth control is forbidden.)

"So Catholics are fed up," she added. "I fault the priests for this, not the people. I think priests have literally betrayed the trust that comes with their holy orders."

A side note here: although the *2007 Yearbook of American and Canadian Churches* rated the Roman Catholic Church as the fastest-growing denomination in the country at 1.94 percent, followed by the Assemblies of God (1.86 percent) and the Mormons (1.63 percent), in-house statistics suggest otherwise. A sobering Catholic News Service story reported in 2006 that although the U.S. Catholic population rose by 1.3 million to 69.1 million that year, the affiliations were in name only. Despite the growth from immigration, the flock was leaving in droves. Church-recognized marriages had dropped by 11,000 in one year, confirmations had dropped by 15,000, first communions had dropped by 40,000, infant baptisms were down by 34,000, and adult confirmations had stayed stable. Also there were 29 fewer priests ordained in 2006 than in 2005. Together with priestly retirements, the number of clergy that year was down by 1,151, and the number of nuns had declined by more than 2,000. Even more troubling for the future was that hundreds of inner-city Catholic schools were closing, especially in the upper Midwest. Although 46 new parishes were started, more churches were closed, resulting in a net loss of 305 parishes. The sex abuse scandals had sent several dioceses into bankruptcy.

Dreher's postscript to his essay on the Lobdell column added that he too had left the Catholic Church over this issue because his very faith was imperiled. He wrote:

> Some people get to the point where they can't believe, no matter how hard they want to or try to force themselves to. Maybe I'm wrong, but I think—I certainly hope—that God grants special mercy to honest men and women like William Lobdell, who have seen more than they can handle. As for

me, I was going the way of William Lobdell because of the Catholic scandal, and the mercy God had for me was in the Orthodox Church. Yet the price I have to pay is never being able to rest in peace in this or any church, ever.

Church as a Time Waster

Near the end of October 2007, I heard of a new book by Rice University sociology professor Michael Lindsay. *Faith in the Halls of Power* is a compendium of 360 in-depth interviews with evangelicals who were at the top of their field in terms of influence and prestige. The book explains how these Christians have lost interest in church because they consider it a waste of their time. These influential people had written off committee meetings that focus on minutiae, incompetent leadership, and inefficient projects. They thought in business terms—long-term planning, strategies, vision, bottom-line performance and progress—concepts that don't exist in church systems run by volunteers and headed by an overworked pastor. Many people in this group were lonely at the top and would have appreciated discussing work issues with their pastor, but, Lindsay writes, ministers are generally clueless about the workaday world.

Intrigued, I called Michael Lindsay.

"These people don't leave the church, but they sort of disengage," he told me. "They are ambivalent. They don't want to be seen as dissing the church, but they feel there's a lack of strong leadership in the local church, and that bothers them. So they decide to do something in the parachurch sector."

As a result, parachurch ministries, such as Young Life or World Vision, flourish because they are efficient, they don't demand a weekly commitment of time, and they have opportunities for people with unusual schedules.

What, I asked Lindsay, should a pastor do?

"Visit parishioners in their place of work," he said. "Pastors are pretty indifferent to that. They don't appreciate work that takes you away from being a Sunday school teacher, elder, or deacon."

I told him about a Christian businesswoman I knew in Washington, D.C., who invited her pastor into town to see the kinds of circles she mixes in. They agreed to meet at a restaurant. When she arrived, she discovered that he had brought along a chaperone. Whereas she saw herself as a professional, he could see her only as a source of temptation. The lunch was a disaster.

He laughed in amazement.

"The typical pastor isn't reaching people at the level where I am interviewing," he said.

There are many, many people out there like those mentioned in Lindsay's book. Used to excellence—or at least efficiency—in the business world, they are hardly going to put up with mediocrity for several hours straight on Sunday mornings. And judging from the many remarks I've collected over the months, people are bored witless at church. Skipping a Sunday doesn't detract from the quality of their week. It may even improve it. Why? Because, they say, they need some time alone with God. Plus, church has nothing to do with their actual lives. What's preached and talked about is irrelevant to their daily existence in the twenty-first century. These are not new believers who haven't yet sunk their roots into the traditions of the church. These are folks converted several decades ago. They see nothing transforming in what's become a dull Sunday morning grind.

Lori Rentzel, a churchless Christian in Petaluma, California, told me of her early days as a believer at the Open Door, a church she attended in the 1970s. Hers was a Pentecostal

Christian culture where it was considered natural to cast out demons, engage in spiritual warfare, or pray for supernatural healing, sometimes all in one morning.

"Those were the days when you never wanted to miss church because so much was going on," she said. "I had my first child on a Tuesday and I was in church that next Sunday. That was the kind of place it was."

Rentzel was leadership material. She spent several years ministering in ex-gay circles, having cowritten the 1994 book *Coming Out of Homosexuality* as well as the 1990 *Emotional Dependency*, both for InterVarsity Press. But none of the churches she tried after Open Door inspired a similar passion in her, much less moved her to contribute her talents.

"Church seems to be a preset mold and either you fit into it or not," she told me. "I want to go back. But it takes such a lot of effort to go there after working all week and doing errands all Saturday. And if you do go, you want something back. You need your batteries charged. Open Door was like that. But church is not like that anymore. You get no return for what you put into it."

As for homosexuality, she added, "I knew people who put their whole selves into trying to change. Some moved on and were able to marry and have seemingly normal lives, but others never could. I no longer have judgment against people who cannot 100 percent pull it off."

The Clueless Church

So, what's happening now? People a generation younger than Rentzel are creating their own wineskins instead of dealing with the current structures. Although they do not consciously strive to be relevant, they are in the middle of where people's lives and needs are. To survive and discern, they must keep an ear to the ground.

In 2000 Lauren F. Winner, then a senior editor for *Christianity Today*, wrote a tell-all column on "evangelical whores" that appeared on Beliefnet, at the time a fairly new multi-religious website. Winner, a fairly recent convert to Christianity from Orthodox Judaism, had written a potboiler of a piece suggesting that unmarried Gen X evangelical Christians often sleep together and that the rest of the evangelical world needed to deal with this. Married evangelicals, she wrote, aren't willing to talk about sex to their single friends, "except to remind us that 'true love waits.' This slogan," she continued, "might work when you're fifteen. Ten years later, catchphrases don't really do the trick."

She went on to describe how the typical church is clueless about the sexual temptations that flourish about the marketplace. Well-meaning preachers use platitudes, if they say anything at all, to remind their singles to stay celibate. More often than not, she said, pastors ignore the "thousands" of unmarried evangelicals who disobey this injunction.

Why, Winner asked, can't we talk about this reality?

The evangelical response to Winner was livid. *Christianity Today* quickly demoted her to a staff writer spot when people started asking why such a recent convert in her early twenties and still in grad school had managed to attain senior writer status at such a revered publication. *World* magazine ran a highly critical article, to which CT executive editor David Neff replied by admitting Winner's ideas were "poorly expressed and therefore easily misunderstood." The author herself responded to *World*'s piece by saying, "I do believe that there should be some place where I, and other singles, can acknowledge the desire for sexual relationships and, in the context of rich church tradition and in the company of older Christians, try to figure out what we can do about it."

I was intrigued by the whole argument, as I had started freelancing for *Christianity Today* years before at the age of twenty-two and had written a lot on single Christians and sexuality. During a business trip to New York, Lauren and I met for dinner at an Upper East Side restaurant near Columbia University, where she was studying. Behind the zany cat's-eye glasses was a woman who asked me searching questions about how I had weathered years of unexpectedly prolonged singleness.

A year later I was lecturing on sexuality issues at Covenant College near Chattanooga, Tennessee. I passed out Winner's Beliefnet essay, along with at least a dozen others on chastity, to the eighteen-year-olds in class. When I asked them which of the pile of reading assignments they liked the best, they preferred Winner's piece. Lauren Winner, they said, was telling it like it is. In spite of all the well-meaning, adult-run abstinence campaigns, many young Christians had already chosen their path. They might stay virgins for now, they said, but if the wait got too long, all commitments were off. Being told to wait had become the default message in much of Christian teaching—even though it was not a major theme in any of Jesus's lectures. Also they told me they weren't hearing many convincing reasons for staying chaste.

Agree with her or not, Winner was relevant in a church culture where pastors may be preaching about events in 2 Kings, but their listeners are more often than not obsessing about the seven deadly sins. Sexual issues are especially tough. People are not taught that it is possible to live up to Christianity's high standards, and so they drift off out of shame or frustration.

"I think of Mark, a single Christian businessman," wrote Stanton L. Jones in a 1993 *Christianity Today* piece on homosexuality. "He oftentimes feels that he lives a twilight existence in the church—a church that does not know how to relate to single people, that acts in revulsion to the very idea of someone being homosexual, a church where he is pestered repeatedly as to why he does not marry, a church in which he longs for intimate fellowship but in which the opportunities for honesty are few and far between."

"A lot of churches do not want to deal with the sexual chaos in a lot of singles' lives," mused Brian McLaren in an interview. "They are not dealing with the messiness of life." The popular author is founding pastor of Cedar Ridge Community Church in Maryland, whose membership is about 50 percent single.

Christian publications especially show an unrealistic delicacy when dealing with sexual matters, substituting terms such as *physical intimacy* for the word *sex* or *the male organ* for *penis*. Kevin Offner, the Washington head of InterVarsity Christian Fellowship, met this challenge head-on by starting meetings for college-aged men to discuss lust and Internet porn. His first group grew to five. A second group he started drew six men.

"These weekly gatherings have been very powerful," Kevin wrote in his personal newsletter in the summer of 2006. "The degree of honesty, frankly, has surprised me. There's something freeing about being able to name a sin publicly and then hear an audible word of forgiveness. I've also been amazed at how prevalent Internet porn is with guys."

The genius of Offner's groups is that he's dealing with issues relevant to the American male. Although the comments on sexual issues by Christianity's founder were comparatively few, he was ultrarelevant to his day and age in other matters.

The constant agricultural metaphors, the dressing-down of the Pharisees, the dealings with the hard cases—prostitutes, lepers, and the demon-possessed—were the things that drew crowds of thousands to follow Jesus.

The Young Are Bailing Out

When church isn't relevant, the first out the door are usually the young. By mid-2006, evangelical youth leaders were complaining about this exact trend. At a series of leadership meetings in forty-four cities, more than six thousand pastors were told that at the current rates, only 4 percent of America's teens will end up as Bible-believing Christians, compared to 35 percent of the baby boomers and 65 percent of their World War II–era grandparents. There was some incredulity shown at the 4 percent figure, which came from a poll commissioned in the mid-1990s, but the consensus was that youth are hardly pouring into church these days, certainly not at the level baby boomers did during the 1970s Jesus Movement. Churches then weren't any more seeker-friendly than they are today, yet there was a revival happening and many churches were transformed by the arrival of legions of hippies and other young people driven to seek God.

Such a spiritual wave is not happening now. In March 2006 the National Association of Evangelicals passed a resolution bemoaning "the epidemic of young people leaving the evangelical church" and an "unacceptably low percentage" of young people who by the age of twenty have made a personal commitment to Christ. This, the resolution added, has "significant implications for the future of the church."

I interviewed Scott McConnell, associate director for Lifeway Christian Resources, the research division for the

Southern Baptist Convention, about what America's largest Protestant denomination was experiencing.

"Our leaders are talking about this exact issue," he said. "Church after church sees seniors graduate and they know they're not in church. I'm picking up on a bit of a revival in some churches aided by [megachurches like] the Willow Creeks and the Saddlebacks to some extent. But as to seeing a movement in our culture today, I don't see that at all."

When the *Wittenburg Door*, a Christian satire magazine, snagged Steve Mansfield (author of *The Faith of George W. Bush* and *The Faith of the American Soldier*) for an interview, one of the first things he did is point out how the young are forsaking church.

"If we're going to talk about the church today, let's be really blunt," he said. "People are voting with their feet. The next generation is not going to church. For the most part, they are going to the First Church of Starbucks. The future of the church is five people over a latte studying a copy of the Purpose Driven something or other. In fifteen years, present trends continuing, the church in America will be half of what it is."

This was from a man who used to pastor Belmont Church in Nashville, a not insignificant two-thousand-member congregation.

In his most recent book, *Secrets in the Dark*, Frederick Buechner tells of how his entire family went to church when he was a child, but whatever they found there didn't touch their real lives. Nor did anything said or done there prevent his father from killing himself when Buechner was ten. One of his uncles also committed suicide a few years later, and his grandfather, he said, died of a broken heart.

"Much of what goes on in churches, I'm afraid," he wrote, "is as shallow and lifeless as much of its preaching and as irrelevant to the deep needs of the people who come to church hungering for a sense of God's presence that they more often than not never find."

The people who are not in church are often "traditional, Bible-believing Christians," wrote Arthur Farnsley, a fellow at the Center for the Study of Religion and American Culture at Purdue University. He described this cohort in a piece for *Christianity Today* about the merchants at Indiana's flea markets, most of whom were living on incomes of less than ten thousand dollars a year. However, many of them believe the Bible is the literal Word of God. They also work two jobs, don't have a lot of free time on their hands, and find church to be a time waster on the one day of the week they do take off. In other words, "They simply do not like church," Farnsley wrote. They are noninstitutional, he said, the gypsies living on the edges of American society.

Farnsley surfaced in a *USA Today* article in early 2008, talking about yet another Lifeway survey of 1,402 unchurched adults, conducted in mid-2007, that said more than 1 in 5 (22 percent) of Americans say they never go to church. That is the highest number ever recorded by the General Social Survey, conducted every two years by the National Opinion Research Center at the University of Chicago, said the article, which compared the two surveys. In 2004 the unchurched percentage was 17 percent.

"So much of American religion today is therapeutic in approach, focused on things you want to fix in your life," he was quoted as saying. "The one-to-one approach is more attractive. People don't go to institutions to fix their problems. Most people have already heard the basic Christian message. The question for evangelism now is: Do you have a take that is authentic and engaging in a way that works for the unchurched?"

One church that did have such a message was a biker's outreach I visited twenty years ago in the blue-collar suburb of Channelview, twenty miles east of Houston. That was when I was at the *Houston Chronicle,* and I had heard of this group that met in a garage that smelled of motor oil rather than incense. The offering was taken in bowl-shaped pan-head valve covers.

But their worship was passionate, refreshing, Pentecostal, and relevant to millions of bikers unreached by traditional churches. Every April they sponsored an outreach known as Biker Sunday that drew hundreds of non-Christians. Since many bikers had spent time in jail, the church also had a lively prison ministry. One of the men I interviewed, Ben Priest, aimed to reach "outlaw bikers," bikers on the run from the law, with the gospel. He began attending their rallies and had had guns pulled on him several times for his pains.

"The outlaw biker don't understand brotherhood or unity," he said. "Society don't want nothing to do with them and they don't want nothing to do with society." But he added, "The heartbeat of the Lord is to evangelize the world. You don't have to be fancy or pretty to do it."

Allen Moorhead, a church member there the night I was conducting interviews, agreed that most churches want nothing to do with bikers. "People think bikers are the scum of the earth, but they're not; they're a sensitive group of people," he said. "A lot of bikers would die for each other. I wish Christians would do that."

What were these people on to? I logged onto Priest's website (www.tribeofjudah.com) and noticed he was following several clear biblical dictates: to evangelize the lost, to operate in the power of the Holy Spirit, and to welcome the miraculous.

In today's postcharismatic era, it's hard to find such a group on American shores. The closest I've gotten in recent years was this church east of Washington, D.C., that caught my attention in the summer of 2006. They had called my office asking me to do a story on a wedding of two formerly homeless people. The day a photographer showed up, it was the rainiest, coldest November morning imaginable. At 6:30 a.m. volunteers pushed off for one of several shelters downtown. It was tough, unglamorous work, cajoling the homeless into a white school bus and back to a church for a few hours of an upbeat service, a warm place in which to sit, and a hot breakfast of grits and muffins. These folks were doing the work that many churches only talk about. One of the former homeless crack addicts, Tuesday Brown Robinson, not only got her life together and married one of the men she met at church (hers was the wedding I was asked to cover), but she now goes out with the bus, poking her face into some of the crack houses where all her friends live. Many of the other volunteers were also once homeless.

By the time the 11 a.m. service rolled around, the pews at From the Heart: Back to Basics Church in Forestville, Maryland, were filled mostly with black men, a demographic that you rarely see in most congregations. The founding pastor, Milt Matthews, and his wife, Linda, gave them a message filled with hope.

"Isn't this what Christianity is supposed to be about?" he asked me just before the service. "Aren't we supposed to be seeking the lost, helping the poor, and getting people functional? If we can't change people, then why are we Christians?"

It took Matthews a few years to get the street savvy he needed to minister on Washington's mean highways and byways. He and his volunteers told me not to believe the homeless who hoist signs saying they are hungry; actually there are so many food giveaway programs in town that no one who truly needs food does without. I asked him how to talk with a homeless person.

"Next time you see someone out there with a sign, you think, *What an opportunity for life.* Spend some time with the brother," he said. "Ask him, 'Why are you here? Do you want Jesus? There's a better life, you know.'"

Like Offner with the college crowd, the church has a Saturday morning men's meeting that deals with sexual issues.

"Those sessions aren't for the weak of stomach," said Wayne Smith, the minister who leads the meeting. "We let it all hang loose. We deal with guys who've been incarcerated and drug users. They're without their children and wives. They've got men's needs. We give them a different way of expressing themselves as Christian men."

In other words, these men are not given the kind of bromides and platitudes that so many Christians hand out to suffering people. When people have walked the same road, they are able to minister to them.

When Christianity Is Attractive

I found some other trendsetters on a late summer day in 2006 at Washington's National Press Club. Appearing before journalists were Red Letter Christians, a new group from the evangelical left that said they were bent toward following the actual words of Jesus as written in red type in certain editions of the Bible. Although the implication from the press conference was they were being faithful to Jesus's true intent, whereas the evangelical right was not, my aim was not so much to chart the continuing jockeying for position as to who is truly worthy of the evangelical mantle but to meet Shane Claiborne.

Claiborne, who had just turned thirty-one, is a 1995 graduate of Eastern University, an evangelical school just west of Philadelphia. In the intervening eleven years, he'd helped found Simple Way, a Christian community in downtown Philadelphia; traveled to Iraq for three weeks in 2003 to protest the war; spent a summer working alongside Mother Teresa in Calcutta; staged demonstrations in Philadelphia's Love Park on behalf of the homeless (and been arrested and jailed for his pains more than once); and lived with the homeless in an abandoned cathedral to prevent police from evicting them. Eventually he ended up on the cover of the September 2005 issue of *Christianity Today*, and a few months later, his first book, *The Irresistible Revolution*, rolled off the presses.

Still trying to live the simple lifestyle, Claiborne showed up at the press conference in his trademark brown bandanna and khaki baggy pants and tunic. His group is snowed under with requests by people who want to come visit, spend time hanging out, join the community, or at least interview them. He listed several prestigious media organizations he had turned down because it was too hard to have an authentic life in a poor neighborhood with television cameras in tow.

It's not so much what Jesus and his disciples said, but how they lived that was so compelling, he told me. "We're giving visibility to Christianity as a way of living rather than as just a way of believing," he said. "I think that is attractive to people. Most people who've been suffocated by doctrine know there's more to Christianity than just believing. When people see there are ways of living that don't conform to the patterns of the world, that is very attractive.

"So we try to live in a way that is magnetic and let it speak for itself. Where the rubber hits the road is how Christians live."

After Shane came back from Iraq, *Spin* magazine showed up at his door and wrote him up. Simple Way got flooded by letters from non-Christians fascinated by the type of Christianity Shane was living out.

"The world is thirsty for another way of life," Shane wrote in his book. "Our culture is starving for answers, as the old ones have gone bankrupt."

About six weeks after the Claiborne interview, I was seated high up in one of Salt Lake City's few skyscrapers. A group of journalists was watching *The Bible Experience*, a preview of an audio dramatization of the Bible, done by an all-black cast. It was pegged as the first multimedia faith-based product that spoke to the culture since *The Ten Commandments*. Those doing the readings were famous speakers and movie stars with just a sprinkling of preachers. It's something the iPod generation could listen to en route to school.

"These are multimedia icons," explained one of the producers, Louis Buster Brown. "It's Christian but it's not corny. The attempt is to engage the culture, then lead them into righteousness."

I liked the idea of an all-black cast, and I lingered to chat with him about that and ways to reach urban youth.

"Young people don't resonate with what is being presented to them in church," he told me. "Eighty percent of the U.S. population is faith-based, but only 18 percent go to church. So where are they getting their faith content? We wanted to provide that."

The Bible Experience rocketed to success, selling two hundred thousand copies within three months of its release. It's a great example of relevancy done right. Urban youth could relate to Bible verses voiced by someone with the same skin color as theirs.

But for the most part, the heavy-duty issues—racism, sexuality, even heresy—are not dealt with. Undeserved suffering, intractable situations, unanswered prayer, and the quiet discouragement of millions of Christians—these elephants in the church living room are left to sit there. But if the church won't bring them up, others will. Just as I was finishing final work on this manuscript, a new book, *God's Problem: How the Bible Fails to Answer Our Most Important Question— Why We Suffer*, showed up on my desk at work. The writer, University of North Carolina professor Bart Ehrman, has turned his rejection of Baptist faith into a cottage industry, pumping out several bestsellers on what's wrong with Christianity. I've no doubt this book will also do well.

On a personal note, I have been perplexed by the suffering I either have encountered as a reporter or reluctantly have had to deal with in my own life. I've seen too many people who feel alienated from God due to exhaustion, depression, sin, or just discouragement. They need to reconnect, and this is the reason I've turned to the books of Bob Sorge, a teacher out of Kansas City who was an up-and-coming Pentecostal pastor and worship leader when a botched throat surgery in 1992 resulted in the near-total loss of his voice. Like the victims of dark fairy-tale enchantments who are given one hour a day to be their true selves, Sorge's throat can at best manage one hour a day of speech before horrific pain sets in. On the day I interviewed him in 2003 at his home in Lees Summit, Missouri, he spent that hour with me. His writings on suffering and why God afflicts people or chooses to allow evil to happen are the best I have found today in contemporary Christian literature.

In a recent book, *Unrelenting Prayer*, he went through a list of thoughtless responses people have given to him on how he should get used to being voiceless. He related those suggestions to the compromises Pharaoh offered Moses in Exodus 10 to get him to stop insisting the Egyptians allow the Israelites to take their children and livestock with them on their exodus.

"These kinds of offers ring in the ears of God's saints all the time," he wrote, "especially to those who are holding out for the manifestation of God's promises in their lives. But like Moses, we won't be comforted until we have received everything for which we are contending. Because Moses refused to be comforted with anything less, he got it all."

In the dark agony of his soul, Sorge has poured out several books on why God allows suffering and practical ways of dealing with it, while awaiting deliverance. That is what's relevant these days. These are books people want to read; these are the kinds of sermons people will attend church to hear.

3

◇◇◇◇◇◇◇

SEARCHING FOR COMMUNITY

What We Really Wish Church Could Be

It was a cold, wet, early fall in Paris in September of 1975 when I visited the Jeu de Paume with a group of students. I was a college sophomore ready to begin a semester abroad in France. We were touring this famous Impressionist museum with our art professor when we noticed a man about our age, wearing a Purdue University T-shirt, listening in. He asked if he could follow along.

After my professor finished the tour and various members of our group dispersed for the afternoon, I began talking with David VanZandt, then in his early twenties and not only an American but an evangelical Christian at that. He had just come back from L'Abri, a ministry in the mountains of French-speaking Switzerland, founded in 1955 by the late theologian Francis Schaeffer.

Four months later I was in Geneva with about ten days to kill. I had plans to meet some friends in Interlaken, but

I wanted to check out this L'Abri place first. I looked up "Schaeffer, Francis," in the phone book and found the number for Chalet Les Melezes, the welcoming point for this evangelical Shangri-la. The person answering the phone said I could come by and gave me some sparse directions. A few hours later, I was standing on the doorstep of this amazing place.

L'Abri, which has centers in Switzerland, the Netherlands, Great Britain, South Korea, Boston, Minnesota, and Canada, is a place where one receives training in some facet of Christianity or, if a skeptic, gets to ask questions about the faith in a quasi-academic setting. I was put to work dusting around the lovely chalets overlooking the looming Swiss Alps and the jagged Dent du Midi mountain. Afternoons I spent listening to tapes on Christianity and pop culture. Meals were delicious and intellectual feasts as well. One spent hours discussing some theological point, and my best conversations with people happened while drying the dishes. There were college-age Christians from all over the world, and living there was like briefly inhabiting heaven. After four months of study in atheistic France, L'Abri was a river of cool water.

Thus, thirty years later, I was intrigued to hear about a research project conducted by Wade Bradshaw, a former staffer with the English L'Abri, as to why so many L'Abri "alumni" had left church. Basically, he told me, these kids could not translate the fellowship and warmth they had found at various L'Abri communities into their local church. When he set up some L'Abri-style fellowships at his own congregation, Trinity Presbyterian in Charlottesville, Virginia, "You would have thought I had invented a new form of space travel," he remarked. "There is such an underlying hunger for this sort of thing." He went on to say that community undergirds people emotionally, and the emotions are where today's spiritual battles are being fought.

"The questions [people are asking] have changed quite significantly in the past thirty years," he said. "It used to be, 'Is there a God?' and now it's 'What I know about God, I don't like.' Their biggest complaint is that God acts in morally inferior ways compared to us." Bradshaw says he can argue this out by asking what the student thinks God should be like, "and then how the God described in Reformed theology fits that."

But even if he answers their theological queries, he's then hit with something altogether different.

"The number one complaint of the American student is, 'I know everything about this gospel but I feel nothing toward it,'" he said. "Anything I offer them that can be interpreted as knowledge or information, they say that no knowledge 'solves the emotional pain that I feel.'"

Emotions can be true or false, Bradshaw will inform them; however, emotional pain is as big an issue with the current twenty-to-thirty-something crowd as was drugs for the baby boomers.

"We of my generation will say, 'What in the world have *you* to complain about?' I was a missionary in Nepal and I saw some real pain," he said. "These kids have everything on one level, but still they have a sense the most important thing is not there. It's not just the gospel as mental assent; they already have that. Propositions do nothing for this generation.

"So like the rich young ruler, I tell them to *do* something. And when they act, faith comes with it. Evangelicals believe belief precedes works, but I have found that works precedes belief."

These were the sorts of questions that could be dealt with in a specialized community like L'Abri, where staff are trained to deal with as attractive an expression of the love of Christ as can be found anywhere, and people long for this type of fellowship.

One of the top reasons people give for their leaving church is loneliness: the feeling—especially in large congregations that no one knows or cares whether they are there. Midweek small groups are a help in creating connections, but fewer and fewer people are able to fight their way through traffic, wolf down dinner, then carve out several hours in a given evening to be part of a small group. The people I talk with who have found true community and then must leave it, due to family or job reasons, pine for it for the rest of their lives.

Church as Supermarket

Jesus's promise to answer any prayer offered by two people agreeing together (see Matt. 18:19) points to living Christianity corporately rather than alone. Christianity is by nature relational, including the provision that one is saved from eternal death by believing on actions performed by someone else, namely, God incarnate.

But the church is not replicating this kind of community, reported pollster George Barna in his 2005 book *Revolution*. And therefore, people are moving on—and moving out of church, as he himself did, joining a house church. Barna wondered if the corporate weekly Sunday service has become passé and suggested believers are now set on forming for themselves what he termed a "personal church of the individual."

The bloggers really went after Barna's book. I saw labels such as "dangerous," "myopic," "autobiographical, not biblical," "beheading Christ," and "church-less Christianity is like sex-less marriage; it lasts one generation." It also got a riposte from Kevin Miller, editor-at-large of *Leadership* magazine: "The phrase 'personal church of the individual' must be the most mind-spinning phrase ever written about the church of Jesus Christ," wrote Miller in *Christianity Today*. He continued:

> Could it be that we evangelical Protestants, who have done more to fragment Christendom than any other group, are now taking that to a logical extreme: a church at the individual level, each person creating a personal "church" experience? At any other point in church history, "personal church" would be nonsensical. In today's America, it's the Next Big Thing.

Perhaps Miller has not experienced churches that make you feel lonelier going out than you felt coming in. Today's church is not the neighborly, participatory place it once was.

In an editorial in the *Dallas Morning News*, then-intern Clint Rainey recounted his thoughts of belonging to one of the area's megachurches that boasts a skate park, sports league, café, game group, and Jumbotrons. He writes that, amid all of the bells and whistles, "we've been reminded interminably, [it] is to 'attract seekers.' I've grown very disenchanted with this concept. Attract seekers to what? A sanctuary worthy of a Broadway production? An auditorium mimicking a convention center? A complex of expensive buildings?"

And do "seeker-friendly buildings" birth seeker-friendly Christians? Rainey is not so sure; in fact the depersonalization and size of churches have resulted in flippant attitudes from the faithful. "As my church has grown," he writes, "so has frequency of cell phone interruptions and families sneaking out early under cover of the dark movie theater environment."

Many churches have become like supermarkets or gas stations: totally depersonalized arenas where most people no longer feel a responsibility to be hospitable to the person standing next to them. At best, during greetings, known as staged "passing of the peace" at some churches, people might shake hands but rarely are names exchanged. It is not the most welcoming atmosphere in which to bring an unsaved friend.

As for those who drop out, no one notices. This factor caught the attention of Lifeway Christian Resources, and they conducted research in 2006 on why people leave churches. "Churches have to keep better track of their people," associate director Scott McConnell told me. "A lot of the formerly churched said no one contacted them after they left. As a church, we at least need to send a message that we noticed you're gone and you're welcome back at any point."

Getting a new person into a small group is key, he said, as small groups are the best places to note when someone has left. But small groups are only doable once the visitor has crossed the threshold several times and decided on a more intense commitment. Most people don't even get to that point.

"If we are to bring these unchurched people into our fellowships, then we must have churches that are structured to meet their needs for friendship and community," wrote one Rodney Gerlack in *Christianity Today*'s letters to the editor section in January 2007. "For centuries, our churches have been sermon and audience focused, where people can go to church and leave with no opportunity for meaningful human contact. Perhaps the early church displayed an answer to this societal need when their meetings were centered around the Lord's

Supper and open sharing and when meetings in homes encouraged the familial nature of the church."

Newer churches have rebranded themselves to reflect this need, wrote Jesse Noyes in the online magazine *Slate*, noting the kinds of places where Christians gather during the Christmas season of 2007 are less apt to have names like "parish," "assembly," or even "fellowship." "Instead they'll gather to celebrate the Advent season in a church whose name expresses universal concepts of community over creed, [like] REUNION, Common Ground, Mosaic, The Gathering, The Table, and Portico."

Disengaged Pastors

Often pastors have problems connecting. This surfaced during the very public downfall of Ted Haggard, who resigned in November 2006 as pastor of New Life Church in Colorado Springs after a male prostitute accused him of soliciting sex and methamphetamines. Haggard was isolated. He had confided in no one about his problems.

Almost one in four Americans have no one to confide in, according to a study published in June 2006 in the *American Sociological Review* by researchers at Duke University and the University of Arizona. Based on interviews with 1,467 people in 2004 and compared to a similar study conducted in 1984, it said the number of close friends for the average American has dropped from three to two. Moreover, people simply aren't signing up for school boards, city councils, PTAs, clubs, bowling leagues, charity activities, and even blood donations.

"This new social detachment appears to have come as a result of our hardwired American pursuit of what we want," columnist Clarence Page wrote about the survey.

We Americans are a restless people who take pride in our autonomy and self-reliance. Rugged individualism, rampant consumerism and restless pursuit of upward mobility and self-reinvention are enduring themes of America's cultural life. . . . Leave it to Americans to come up with the mega-church, where we can stroll in and decide precisely how much we want to be involved in a new community— or stay semi anonymous in the crowd, just you and me, God.

"Natalie," a single mom I talked with in Walla Walla, Washington, put things more bluntly: "There's a fight out there, but no one at church is willing to go to the mat for each other," she said. "Finally you get tired and wonder if God is going to come through for you. The body of Christ is not standing by each other when we have a real need. I've never been at a church where people really pray for each other."

An article in the *Los Angeles Times*, which led with a poll, citing findings that just 17 percent of adults view the local church as essential for developing faith, said the explosion in digitized spirituality might make the local church obsolete. Different forms of technology are allowing Christians to decentralize where they get their spiritual needs met. Instead of in one building for three hours on a Sunday morning, they can find everything from chat groups to teachings on the Internet.

Sitting in a pew on Sunday morning seems almost embarrassingly old-fashioned in an era when you can watch a video recreation of the Last Supper on your Palm or get God's word text-messaged to your cell phone. Bored with your pastor's ramblings? Select a peppier sermon from among hundreds of "godcasts" online. Just pick a topic: Christian dating, Old Testament prophets? Then download it to your MP3 player.

This challenge is not new. The church has been dealing with this issue ever since people decided they got more from staying home Sundays and watching a televangelist than from slogging through the weather to make it to church. The problem is not the high-tech factor; it's the fact that quality material is available to Christians outside the four church walls. The *Times* article closes, in fact, with a tale of a family in Shawnee, Oklahoma, who worship in front of a flat-screen computer monitor at their home by listening to a service going on in Oklahoma City, forty-five miles away.

Acting Out Scripture

Where the church holds the trump card is in human contact, as downloadable sermons are no substitute for friends. People want community, and a few places are going to surprising lengths to create it. Santa Paula, a town profiled in *American Enterprise* as an oasis for conservative, homeschooling Catholics, lies in the heart of what the magazine termed "blue-state, secular, mightily individualistic California." Scattered about the city, an hour's drive north of Los Angeles, is a network of people who help out on child care and support for family emergencies, such as sickness, death, or the birth of a child. They also help each other find jobs.

> Here, no child will be teased for wearing hand-me-down clothes, or think it odd that he has to share a bedroom with his siblings. Here, moms aren't made to feel as though they're "wasting" their education by choosing to raise their kids full time. Here, homeschoolers aren't considered freakish, unsocialized outsiders; they're some of the brightest, nicest kids in town.

There are similar countercultural Catholic clusters in Steubenville, Ohio; Front Royal, Virginia; Ave Maria, Florida; Ann Arbor, Michigan; and South Bend, Indiana, all towns with a nearby university or college. Some of these were once large Christian communities of committed households—often numerous singles bunking in with a nuclear family or singles-only houses—that formed the basis of the Catholic charismatic renewal.

Some friends of mine are trying to start a similar cluster in Hyattsville, just south of the University of Maryland at College Park. They have attracted numerous Catholic families who attend Mass together and whose kids play together while their parents pray the Liturgy of the Hours together on Sunday nights. They've created a Catholic moms group to share homeschooling materials and play dates. They simply wanted a support network of folks who worshiped the same way and didn't hassle them for having lots of children.

Other friends are slowly building up a community of former evangelicals who've joined Holy Cross, an Orthodox parish just south of Baltimore. Congregants make a point of sharing the sacramental bread with guests, and anyone who hangs about the place after the service will be invited to a very sociable potluck in the downstairs hall. Many parishioners have moved to within a short driving distance. This idea is not limited to Christians; Orthodox Jews have long clustered in certain neighborhoods in Brooklyn for the support, friendship, and need to be within walking distance of a synagogue on the Sabbath. If one wants to preserve a culture, geographic closeness is key.

I learned this while writing about a small Episcopal church in east Houston that became a world-famous parish in the 1960s and 1970s. Located not far from the main campus of the University of Houston, Church of the Redeemer was fresh into the charismatic movement of the 1960s. The place had that alluring quality that inspired people to give up their cars for someone more needy than themselves, lay aside their careers for the good of the vision of the church, and in one case, bake a chocolate cake for the neighbors who were vandalizing their car. (The vandalizing stopped.) Cars, houses, and possessions changed hands many times, as members copied what they saw the church's leaders doing. "The Holy Spirit," an elder named Bob Eckert told me in an interview, "has to be careful of what he reveals to us because that's what we'll do."

The all-important ingredient in this venture is that everyone lived within a half mile of each other in the same seedy neighborhood and had a bird's-eye view of what was happening out on the streets. They discovered a widow, Essie Ringo, who had twenty-two adopted children, plus an invalid mother to care for in a three-bedroom bungalow. The Eckerts and their four boys had fourteen women living with them, crammed into a six-bedroom house. Sure enough, Bob Eckert and his wife, Nancy, began to hear the Lord directing them to "give" their home to Essie, furniture and all. They did not move out; they planned to walk out, relocating to another, smaller dwelling that had merely a stove and a refrigerator. Three days before the move, they got a call from another church member who had a houseful of extra furniture. Could she store it at the Eckerts' new house?

There was a lot of this sort of thing in the 1960s and 1970s, not only in Houston but in like-minded Christian communities in Ann Arbor, Chicago, South Bend, and many other locales. I met people who, instead of church hopping in search of the best spiritual bargain, had given up job promotions and transfers to stay put for the sake of their church. It was considered sinful to bail out simply because one disagreed with the service or the pastor. People at Redeemer and similar places were exhorted to go to all lengths to work out thorny relationships instead of bolting. As a result, the unity and love in many of these communities was palpable, drawing thousands of visitors who just wanted to soak up the atmosphere.

But anyone familiar with the history of the Christian communities that sprang forth in the 1960s and 1970s is aware of the high cost of belonging to one of them. Many demanded a high financial commitment and every moment of one's free time. Many slipped into an authoritarian mold that wiped out their many benefits. Today's evangelicals are seeking something a little less personally costly: house churches.

The Twenty-First-Century House Church

George Barna, founder of the influential Barna Group, has bought into the current house-church trend. According to a massive Barna survey in June 2006 of five thousand people, 9 percent of all American adults are involved in a house-church gathering. Since these are otherwise known as small groups, shepherd groups, home Bible studies, and the like, the statistic is not too surprising. Extrapolated, this means twenty million adults attend some sort of gathering in a home once a week. Over the course of a month, that number jumps to forty-three million.

This is not a huge trend so far. Of the adults surveyed, 74 percent just attend a conventional church, and 19 percent attend both—Sunday services at their church and a midweek meeting in a home. (The other 2 percent attend a small group that's not categorized as a house church.) The really interesting group to watch is the 5 percent who attend just a house church. The groups most likely to attend a house church come from some of the biggest unreached segments of America—minorities, men, and residents of the West. Homeschooling families also like these gatherings. Barna is betting that more and more adults will adopt such meeting places as their primary faith community, buttressed by a spiritual smorgasbord of Christian radio, books, listservs, and websites.

In fact Barna hosts a house church. *Revolution*, which announced that some twenty million evangelicals were leaving the traditional church for greener pastures, was a manifesto for this movement. *Revolution*, he told *Charisma* in 2006, brought more negative and positive feedback than any of his thirty-seven previous books.

I spoke with Barna in July 2007 and asked him how he was liking his house-church experience.

"We're loving it," he said. "It's the best thing we've ever done. What it has done for the families involved is helped us not just to attend church together. Everyone in the church is really involved. We really look out for each other. It is one big extended family of twenty-three people."

One unusual facet of this group is that they have substituted a regular meal for a bread-and-wine Holy Communion ceremony. "The ceremonial thing that most churches do—that is something that was kind of made up," he said. "That was not the original way Christians did it. Communion for them was having a meal together."

I questioned him on this point. Jesus and his followers had already finished eating a meal when he swung into this new rite based on wording from the Jewish Passover liturgy.

"But was he saying that we should do this exact thing each time?" Barna asked me. "No," he answered.

I met with him again in September during a trip to Los Angeles, and house churches, he assured me again, are absolutely the way to go.

The Good and the Bad

Typical of the kind of people who join a house church are Diane and Emile, she a sculptor and he a playwright in Norfolk, Virginia, a highly evangelical/Pentecostal area that draws much energy from nearby Regent University in Virginia Beach.

They were tired of how every church they entered was involved in some kind of building project. "Why is small bad?" Diane asked as we chatted in an ethnic restaurant near one of her art shows. "Why does everyone want to be the Crystal Cathedral?"

In mid-2006 they began attending a house church that met Sunday morning in a home, finishing with a potluck lunch. They liked the unplanned nature of the meeting; sometimes someone would prepare a study; another time someone would bring up a moral dilemma and those present would offer up the Scriptures that deal with the situation. Whereas many pastors are uncomfortable leaving a discussion un-resolved, participants in a house-church meeting don't feel they have to end sermon times with answers.

"A lot of us came from churches that were controlling," Diane said, "so we were all sensitive to that. And I hated the politics and the backbiting."

The conversation flowed toward evangelical friends we knew who had gone Catholic or Orthodox. Emile, whose background was Antiochan Orthodox, had toyed with the idea of joining such a church. One thing that appealed to them was the God-centeredness of the typical Orthodox service—both Emile and Diane disliked churches that catered heavily to children. Orthodox liturgies were not focused on children—or anyone, for that matter—other than God. The Orthodox, Emile said, are answering the question no one is asking: what is the true church?

"The true church," Emile concluded, "is when two or three people get together." So, to date, Emile has not gone the route of the Orthodox Church. To these artistically sensitive people, their group feels organic and freeing. They attend to fulfill their desire rather than their obligation.

For many, the flexibility and accountability of these groups is appealing, plus the feeling of belonging; if you are not at a gathering, everyone notices it. Often this is not so at an ordinary church. And if one's small group provides emotional and prayer support, mentoring and Bible study, what is there for the larger church to provide? The latter demands a tenth of one's salary and takes up a chunk of one's Sunday. If the worship is so-so, well, do the math. More and more people are concluding there's really no reason to go.

In mid-2006 *Charisma* had listed twenty books that dealt with the new house-church movement. Near the end of the year, the Religion Newswriters Association, an organization for reporters in the secular media, posted a long list of interview possibilities for articles on the trend. If this movement has this kind of substantial research available, it's got legs.

In January 2007 Barna's organization released an update specifying the higher levels of satisfaction people felt with their house churches as compared to people attending a regular church. Barna is fairly partisan, as he rates people who are still in regular churches as "spiritually complacent," compared with those who are attracted to house churches. The latter are either young adults interested in spirituality and faith but not in the organized church or baby boomers who are seeking a deeper and more intense experience with God and other believers, the update said.

Typically, house-church attendees who were "completely satisfied" with the teachings, leadership, and community of their group were in the sixtieth percentile, as compared to those in regular churches, who polled in the fortieth percentile. House-church meetings are usually on a Sunday or Wednesday and last two hours. Of those who attend such groups, Barna found:

- 93 percent have spoken prayer during their meetings
- 90 percent read from the Bible
- 89 percent spend time serving people outside of their group
- 87 percent devote time to sharing personal needs or experiences
- 85 percent spend time eating and talking before or after the meeting
- 83 percent discuss the teaching provided
- 76 percent have a formal teaching time
- 70 percent incorporate music or singing
- 58 percent have a prophecy or special word delivered
- 52 percent take an offering from participants that is given to ministries
- 51 percent share communion
- 41 percent watch a video presentation as part of the learning experience

The average size of these groups is twenty people; 64 percent include children and there is an average of seven children under the age of eighteen involved, which shows that the traditional church does not have a lock on the family demographic.

The downside of this movement is that just because people meet in a home doesn't mean there are always treasures of fellowship and teaching to be had there, and house churches aren't always the panacea they are reputed to be. For several years I've been tracking the progress of two of my Portland, Oregon, friends in finding a church. "Evan" and "Emily" had attended the same informal fellowship as I had years before at Lewis and Clark College in the southwest part of town. Once we graduated, though, it was a rude shock attending most churches, where there was little welcome compared to our close-knit college group. For years they've tried various churches and even no church for a while until Evan—more than Emily—began to feel that God does require Christians to be in some sort of fellowship.

"I have become convinced through my New Testament studies that I have to participate in church, even though I don't like parts of it," Evan said. "If you go back to the Pentateuch, God is calling people to be his own possession. And we're baptized by one Spirit into the body of Christ. The body may be imperfect, but I cannot opt out of it and not participate in it. I've emphasized the personal elements of salvation in the past, but now I'm emphasizing more the corporate."

So they began attending, albeit reluctantly, a small fellowship meeting in a home.

"Most of us don't fit into the standard 'churchianity,'" Emily said. "Early on, the church was much more what Evan and I had envisioned. We called ourselves a 'church of misfits,' and that was true. At the beginning, we shared a lot. It was not unusual to interrupt the sermon and ask a question and have a discussion before going back to the sermon. But we don't do that anymore. It's become more the kind of church we don't like—the same routine every week that becomes your liturgy."

"We are leaving door-hangers around the neighborhood to get people to come to church," Evan said. "We shouldn't have to be doing that. We have also begun to think of what it takes to have a growing church, and we are getting into the nonspiritual aspects of a corporate church. Now we're starting to look at land to build on."

As the house church formalized, it moved to a nearby school, which took much of the informal charm out of the gathering. The fellowship was good, the worship so-so, and the teaching erratic in terms of addressing any of their issues, such as the death of Emily's father awhile back. Emily wanted out, but Evan wanted to hang in there.

"I want to have a positive influence, so I am working within my own church to make sure it's biblically oriented," he said. "One reason why churches don't satisfy is they don't take the gospel seriously. They don't seem relevant in that they're not really helping me figure out how to live in a way that is glorifying God in contemporary society. Some churches we have been to don't do much for others. Some of the newer postmodern churches are better in that area, even though they take the Word a bit too lightly."

My heart went out to them. I had visited their house church during one of my visits to Portland, and I had to agree the teaching was not its strong point. Finally, I learned their little group had taken steps to associate with the Southern Baptists. This sent my friends back out the door.

"We are now churchless," said Emily's last email, "starting to look for a place that is a better fit—sigh. Perhaps the impossible dream. Yes, the church seemed to be going more toward churchianity. . . . We love the people at the old church, just not the direction the church was headed."

My own experience with small groups might be instructive. During my postcollege years, I lived in a Christian community near Portland State University where we pooled salaries and lived very simply. I was never lonely there, and the companionship, the many meals together, and the worship were wonderful. In 1979 I was able to visit Reba Place Fellowship, a similar Mennonite community in Evanston, Illinois, and the Episcopal Community of Celebration near Colorado Springs a year later to see what things were like in these communities. During that same period, I became a correspondent for a community newsletter, visiting and reporting on Christian communes around the Pacific Northwest. All of these places were inhabited by Christians who wanted to do something radical with their lives. They were people who didn't just want polite greetings on a Sunday morning; they wanted to share their lives.

Eventually I left community and joined churches with small groups. But, the longer I was a believer and the more complicated life became, the less helpful home groups were for me. My book on sexual purity (*Purity Makes the Heart Grow Stronger*) was written partly because I had no one at church to confide in about such matters, and I figured many readers out there were in the same boat. My small group was of absolutely no help. Also I had questions on how to maintain integrity amid a dog-eat-dog journalistic setting. I was battling management over some issues, but no one in my small group knew how to advise or help me. Very few of the people there understood the business world, much less the backstabbing nature of a typical newsroom. Years later, when I moved to Washington, I quickly became part of a specialty group for Christians in the media. Soon, though, when I ended up on their board and in charge of the local chapter, I was mentoring others, not receiving the ministry I needed.

The idea behind small groups in a church is that leaders provide the major pastoring, freeing up the senior pastor for other things. But many small-group leaders I have met over the years have no discernment, pastoring, or teaching gifts whatsoever. And I find myself wondering, *How is the emerging house-church movement any different?* I understand that it has been born out of frustration with what the institutional church has become. People join informal small groups rather than do without any fellowship at all. But if in general the leadership is as poor as in many of the groups I've had contact with, I predict house churches will be a short trend. If they manage to create vibrant, life-changing, supernaturally endowed community, they will last.

4

◇◇◇◇◇◇◇◇

EMERGENCE AND RESURGENCE

Adjusting to the Twenty-first Century

It was a breezy, sun-swept summer morning in Seattle, one of those crystal-clear days that show off the glittering mountain ranges both east and west of the city. Just north of the city's Ballard district, a klatch of people were gathered in the parking lot of a one-story slate-gray building. Meeting in a former auto parts store at 14th and Leary Way, Mars Hill Church is a flagship congregation in the largely unchurched Pacific Northwest. Just a few blocks from a ship channel and a ten-minute drive from the University of Washington, with a student body of thirty-nine thousand, the church's courtyard was filled with twenty-somethings on their cell phones plus hordes of families with young children.

I was there to track one of several congregations that were successfully going outside the box in terms of ministering to twenty-first-century young adults; people not known for their church attendance. Mars Hill's entrance was unassuming: two glass doors leading into a tiny vestibule. Wandering about, I saw informally dressed female ushers, a coffee bar near the west entrance for the Starbucks deprived, and a dimly lit sanctuary with black upholstered seating and no windows.

A rock band, Brothers of the Empty Tomb, comprised of young men dressed in black, was blaring as announcements were flashed on a huge screen. Suddenly the music switched to a heavy rock version of "I'll Fly Away." The congregation was supposed to sing, but the band's volume was so loud, it was impossible to hear any voices. Then we swung into "Testify," another rock selection, and I glanced around. Hardly anyone *was* singing.

Not to worry—worship was not the focal point of this gathering. Within ten minutes, an informally dressed man, whom I surmised was senior pastor Mark Driscoll, approached the mike to launch a sixty-five-minute sermon on male-female roles in 1 Corinthians 11. I had to ask five people around me before I found someone who knew that this was Driscoll. Clearly there were many visitors in the gathering, but none of the leaders up front introduced themselves.

"I'm going to be clearing up a lot of misunderstandings in the blogosphere on this issue," is how Driscoll began. And a sermon about "chicks and dudes" followed, which got into some pretty deep territory on biblical chivalry, complementarianism, and feminism. His example of gender differences: "My daughters like to go shopping and my sons like to pee in the yard."

The man was certainly hip; not only did he use Google and text-messaging, but he was into leaf blowers and Seattle Mariners games. He kept what would normally be an attention-deficit-driven crowd still the entire time with what was a pretty conservative read on male/female roles. He was not one to favor women as pastors or preachers; instead, women should be modest, feminine, and "not dressed like a hooker," he said, advice some of his female listeners were definitely not keyed into.

He took on Calvin Klein ads for being androgynous and Seattle for being like Corinth in terms of gender confusion. "I almost preached this sermon in a dress to illustrate my point," he said, joking. He spent several minutes telling the men to act like responsible adults. In a slap at a current craze, women who are "shaving their heads and going butch like lesbians," he added, are being "sexually adulterous and inappropriate." His listeners were lapping it up.

Following the sermon there was some soul and blues music and then a quickie celebration of communion that left out the other part of 1 Corinthians 11 (the words reminding the congregation of Jesus's words at the Last Supper). I was still waiting for those verses to be read out loud—as is customary in most churches—when I saw people jump up and line up in front of informally dressed ushers carrying baskets of bread and goblets of either wine or grape juice. There was no liturgy as a reference point for the congregation. A closing prayer included a plea for wives to submit to husbands.

When I visited the church bookstore after the service, I found mostly books by men and only three by women: one on miscarriage, one on women and prayer, and one called *The Excellent Wife*. Later on I would learn via *Christianity Today* that single women were the largest demographic at Mars Hill. Yet there were precious few books for women and no books for singles. Was this overwhelmingly Gen Y crowd just supposed to marry young?

Mars Hill, I surmised, was like attending a website: you log in, lurk for ninety minutes, then log out. People are there to get individual needs met. The unfriendliness of its people (no one greeted me), the odd music, and the movie theater ambiance put me off. If you wanted community, you could inquire about some of the small groups mentioned in the newspaper-style bulletin.

The dark interior was purposely instituted, Driscoll had told us in the sermon, to attract male congregants who get turned off by the feminized setup at many churches. The possibility that all those single female congregants might not like this cocktail lounge atmosphere either didn't occur to anyone or wasn't considered relevant.

Nevertheless, Mars Hill, one of a band of new urban Re-formed congregations springing up around the country, is packing them in, not the least because of Driscoll's impressive preaching. According to the *Christianity Today* piece, the church grew by one thousand people in January 2007 alone. The following September, I was back in Seattle and amazed to see the church's mass baptism at Alki Beach on Puget Sound make the nightly news. Comically, a baby seal had beached itself right where the church held a permit to do some two hundred baptisms. Its mother was frantically swimming offshore. Since there's a hefty fine levied on anyone who touches a stranded seal (sometimes their mothers will not touch a baby that's been handled by humans), the church was in a quandary. About three thousand people were slated to show up at 6:30 p.m. to watch an event that wasn't being allowed to happen. All sorts of media and environmentalists appeared to either take part in or witness the confrontation on that cloudy and chilly Friday afternoon.

After several phone calls to the city, the church was allowed to move a few hundred yards down the beach, as the seal was not budging, despite desperate prayers from the Mars Hill folks. At the last minute, the tide came in, the little seal swam off and rejoined its mother, and all those television, radio, and newspaper reporters standing around ended up reporting on the baptism.

"God-ordained publicity" is how one church member's blog described it.

Movie House Evangelism

Seattle's Mars Hill isn't the only church thinking out of the box. At least one denomination, the Presbyterian Church of America, is pioneering similar congregations for the urban twenty-something who wants a whole different look to worship than what he or she grew up with. They have successfully seeded churches in parts of the city—often highly gay neighborhoods, such as Seattle's Capitol Hill and Washington DC's Dupont Circle—that other evangelical churches avoid.

Mark Driscoll told *Christianity Today* in a 2006 interview that the two "hot theologies" of the first decade of the twenty-first century are Reformed and emerging. He contrasts the two: "Reformed theology offers certainty, with a masculine God who names our sin, crushes Jesus on the cross for it and sends us to hell if we fail to repent," he said. "Emerging theology offers obscurity, with a neutered God who would not say an unkind word to us, did not crush Jesus for our sins and would not send anyone to hell."

According to an October 2006 Barna study, baby busters or Gen Xers—people in their thirties—are a rather immoral lot, hence Driscoll's unbending stance. Compared with baby boomers, secular busters are significantly different from their elders. They are twice as likely to have viewed a sexually explicit movie or video, two and a half times more likely to have sex outside of marriage, and three times more likely to have viewed pornography online. Only three out of ten busters believe in absolute truth; 50 percent say ethics and morals are based on "what is right for the person," compared with one-quarter of the over-forty set.

In the same poll, Barna queried born-again busters. They were less likely to download music illegally, smoke, view porn, purchase a lottery ticket, or use profanity. However, they were more likely to try to get back at someone or to steal something.

The morality of the under-forties set mirrors a society where divorce, crime, single-parent households, and suicide are much more prevalent than thirty years ago when the Boomers grew up. Moral experimentation and what used to be thought of as unusual sexual behaviors are the norm not the exception, and younger people have a more disconnected, individualized, less trusting spin on morality, said David Kinnaman, president of the Barna Group, in remarks released with the poll. "It is important for churches to understand the natural skepticism of busters as well as their desire for spiritual and conversational depth," he said. "Young adults do not want to hear on-the-stage monologues about moral regulations."

With this group, church dropouts tend to be youth who grew up in the church, then tuned out. So how does one minister to the been-there-done-that crowd? One well-known example is National Community Church, a congregation based in a downtown movie theater in Washington DC's majestic, beautifully restored Union Station. I had visited once on a Sunday and was less than taken with the omnipresent smell of popcorn and the general weirdness of trying to worship in a movie house near all those railroad tracks.

The church is pastored by Mark Batterson, who studied at Trinity Evangelical Divinity School in Deerfield, Illinois, and is credentialed with the Assemblies of God. Although his first try at church planting in the Chicago area crashed and burned, his Washington experiment caught on big, starting in 1996, expanding from nineteen people to eleven hundred, attending five services in two local movie theaters.

There was also a Saturday night service that meets at Ebenezers, a coffeehouse barely a five-minute walk from Union Station's marble pillars. Ebenezers was far classier than the movie theater locale. It's a 2.5-million-dollar re-model of a 1908 diner that is now a classy brick-and-glass café. One has to look hard to find the worship space in the basement, as there is no sign pointing out the way to inquir-ers. Unlike 1970s-style Christian coffeehouses, there was no evangelistic literature to be found anywhere, and the souve-nir postcards barely mentioned the church. The downstairs was lined with plush burnt orange and lime green cush-ioned benches. Music lyrics were flashed on mini Toshiba screens; the offering plates were burlap bags. The design of the church's interior was edgy urban with metal piping on the ceilings, acoustic paneling on the walls, and faux railroad track designs on the floor. There was some obvious brand-ing: a wall banner up front bearing the theme of a sermon series, which dovetailed with the title of Batterson's latest book. One of his core convictions, he would tell me later, is "the greatest message deserves the greatest marketing."

Like Mars Hill, the worship was fifteen minutes long, with everything built around the forty-five-minute sermon.

After my first visit, I met with Batterson in his upstairs office. Seventy percent of his congregation had no church to call home or they had opted out of church five to ten years before showing up at National Community Church. "Boring," "irrelevant," or "bigoted" were the words they used to de-scribe how they felt about their past worship experiences.

"We're almost a church for the dechurched," he said. "The Lord has put us here to keep a lot of twenty-somethings from falling through the cracks.

"I am not of the camp that asks what's wrong with our culture," he continued. "I ask why the church is losing 60 percent of our twenty-somethings. Churches are doing mission out of memory, not imagination. It's perceived as having ignored culture and condemned culture, but we want to create a culture."

One way is to adopt the coffeehouse model.

"Coffeehouses are postmodern wells, and we are following in the footsteps of Jesus and meeting at wells," Batterson observed. "I have a sense God is calling the church out of the church. We love the marketplace environment because dechurched and unchurched people are intimidated by a church. People are likely to go to church at a place where they've been before. Everyone's seen a movie at Union Station."

Everyone under thirty also logs on to the Internet, which is why these young people read Batterson's "evotionals" on the Web or download audio feeds of Driscoll's sermons.

This generation tends to be disinterested in church unless they are running it. Barna research indicates only one out of eight churchgoing young people (ages twenty-two to forty) has served as a lay leader during a recent two-year period, compared to one out of four baby boomers (ages forty-one to fifty-nine) and one out of three elders (over sixty).

"The feeling of being sidelined is especially frustrating to young leaders because they actually *want* to grow and learn," Kinnaman said in an article in *Ministry Today* describing their findings. Churches are throwing away a lot of young talent, he said, because the young "do not merely want a period of training and apprenticeship in which they are slowly and methodically nurtured for some distant leadership horizon. Instead, young leaders want hands-on meaningful opportunities."

My own experience in the newspaper business corroborates this. When I was in my twenties, it was expected that one's first few newspaper jobs would be in small towns where one makes all the inevitable mistakes before moving up to the major metro dailies. I was thirty when I got my big break working for the *Houston Chronicle*. My first book came out when I was thirty-two, which was considered precocious at the time.

For the interns I mentor at the *Washington Times*, thirty is somewhere beyond eternity. These young adults switch jobs every year, they want to be working in the big leagues by their midtwenties if not sooner, they wish to kick off their careers in Washington instead of ending them there, and they also want that first book under their belt by the time they turn twenty-five.

Although one could argue that few people have much to say to the world before they hit thirty, it's true that most twenty-somethings think beyond the box. According to David McCullough's book *1776*, George Washington got his most intense training starting as a sixteen-year-old surveyor's apprentice in western Virginia and as a twenty-something fighter in the French and Indian War in the 1750s. When he took charge of the Continental Army in 1775 at the age of forty-three, his youngest general, Nathanael Greene, was just thirty-three. John Hancock, president of the Continental Congress, was thirty-nine, and Thomas Jefferson was thirty-two. Those men had to be trained somewhere before emerging as leaders. Colonel Henry Knox, whose daring three-hundred-mile transport of cannon from Fort Ticonderoga to the hills overlooking Boston was lavishly described in the book, was twenty-five.

But what about the baby boomers, who are just as disenchanted with church? Just before my Seattle visit, I'd dropped by one of the country's top "emergent" churches. Cedar Ridge Community Church, founded in 1982 by Brian McLaren, is nestled next to cornfields in bucolic Maryland. McLaren, who had retired several months earlier, was guest preaching on breaking down oppressive systems and bringing good news to the poor and oppressed. Mentions of Hurricane Katrina were mixed with quotes from Martin Luther King. We prayed sentences like, "Drive us toward a new life of justice, peace, and integrity." It was not your typical evangelical suburban fare.

Although the "emergent church" movement is a huge mixed bag of theologies that usually attracts the young, Cedar Ridge seemed made up of baby boomers who had moved beyond evangelicalism. What they had moved into was hard for me to tell, but the church seemed to be meeting a need.

Conservative and liberal alike are adopting the term *emergent* to describe themselves, so it's safe to say these congregations are a new generation of churches that are works in progress. Their focus is on the creative, the improvisational; as Batterson says, "The church ought to be the most creative place on the planet."

Unlike a lot of suburban churches, Cedar Ridge was racially mixed and made up of about 50 percent singles. I was fifteen minutes late, and the worship portion was already over, the forty-minute sermon already begun. Like Mars Hill, it was dark inside except for some clerestory windows high up.

Unlike Mars Hill, there was a cross visible on an altar and a short explanation about communion being a sacrament. The liturgy was borrowed from the Episcopal Book of Common Prayer. Then we were invited to partake of the bread and wine ourselves and visit one of several stations around the church where we could ask for prayer or light a candle or give an offering, kind of like an ecclesiastical cafeteria. Doctrinal statements were posted in the foyer, free doughnuts and coffee were passed out afterward, and McLaren stuck around up front to greet people.

They also had newcomers come to the front after the service to hear a seven-minute introductory speech and receive a packet explaining the church and its ministries, plus a CD about Cedar Ridge's mission.

In an interview, McLaren told me that low-key is the way to go with the current crowd. "All sorts of fads—*Passion of the Christ*, forty days of purpose—have been marketed to churchgoers," he told me, "so there is a fatigue factor that sets in. It has to do with overpromising results. It is part of the hype of consumer culture, and if it doesn't work, you just move on. Televangelism has turned the whole country into a burned-over district," he added, referring to upstate New York after all sorts of religious movements were birthed there in the midnineteenth century. "Kids grow up in families of wacko-religious parents and so they decide they do not want to be religious."

Marrying the Culture

Then I talked with Evan and Emily, the two Portland, Oregon, believers interviewed in the last chapter, about their visit to a fourth outside-the-box church: Imago Dei Community in the southeast part of town. What they ran into sounded like a mix of Cedar Ridge and Mars Hill.

"We went two Sundays in a row, and both Sundays they were not teaching from Scripture," Emily told me. "One was a guest speaker and another was a topical speaker. The music was pretty unconventional, obviously geared toward reaching a lot of unchurched people."

Both services they attended were packed. Pluses included the church's desire to reach out to groups, such as AIDS patients, that traditional churches don't often get to. Minuses included a general sloppiness among the attendees.

"The people dressed pretty inappropriately for a church," Evan said. "I think churches have to figure out what they are doing on that score."

"It was the hottest day of the summer and some of the girls were dressed in shorts with little left to the imagination," Emily said. "There was a real disconnect there."

"Moreover," she added, "the elements of communion were set out under candlelight, which looked very solemn, but there was wild music going on. There was no explanation of what was going on. So everyone just went and stood in line."

These emergent and new-breed churches seem to have a few kinks to iron out on how to handle the sacraments. Emergents have been criticized for marrying the culture, but they respond that they are on the cutting edge of new realities in culture. They also say Christianity is fast losing its grip on American culture, a thought borne out by a late 2006 survey by George Barna that showed that even the most famous evangelical leaders barely raise an eyebrow among the secular world.

Barna took sixteen public figures—actors, entertainers, and ministers—and found that, although people didn't know the ministers, they definitely knew about actor Denzel Washington, singer Britney Spears, and actor/director Mel Gibson. Bestselling evangelical authors, such as Rick Warren, James Dobson, T. D. Jakes, and Tim LaHaye, barely registered. Two out of three Americans had never heard of Jakes; three out of four had never heard of LaHaye; six out of every ten adults had never heard of Dobson; and as for Warren, whose books have sold twenty-five million copies at this writing, three out of every four adults and two out of every three born-again Christians had never heard of him. Joel Osteen, who heads a megachurch in Houston and is the heir of his father's Pentecostal empire, likewise proved obscure to the general public. However, in 2005, when Osteen visited the MCI Center in Washington, seats sold out fast.

The familiar faces are the movie actors, TV stars, and politicians. The greater the awareness, the greater the influence on people's lives and the access to their minds and hearts.

"You cannot make a difference in someone's life if you do not have entrée in that life," Barna said in remarks attached to the survey. "In our society, even clergy compete for people's attention and acceptance. One of the reasons the Christian faith is struggling to retain a toehold in people's lives is because even the highest-profile leaders of the faith community have limited resonance with the population."

Mars Hill, National Community, Cedar Ridge, and other churches founded in the past quarter century seek to collaborate with culture to evangelize the masses. Their critics are people like Wilbur Ellsworth, the former pastor of First Baptist Church of Wheaton, Illinois, who was ordained an Antiochan Orthodox priest in the spring of 2007. The Orthodox are deliberately retro by fifteen hundred years or more.

"There is a way in which evangelicalism as a broad movement is being too worldly in trying to reach this culture," Ellsworth told me. "In the process, they have become it. They have embraced all kinds of things that have stripped from them the wisdom and tradition of the church.

"For instance, there is the constant call for variety and creativity in worship. The reason they have to be creative is they have to continually think up new things to do. Continually needing to be creative means that you have to keep changing it—and why do you have to change it? Because it's getting old—it's not conveying to the people and conveying a deep recognition that this has enormous cosmic meaning. "

Concerning Orthodoxy, he explained, "Saying these prayers and doing this liturgy is expressing the realities of eternity in this liturgy."

Anyone who has been in an Orthodox church, filled with icons, incense, and priests in ceremonial robes, knows this is an alternate kingdom. Absolutes are preached here, and there are disciplines in place to instill them, such as fasting, venerating icons, and soaking oneself in the sayings and teachings of the early fathers of the church. This is the way all churches should be, Ellsworth said, not what he'd term gimmicky houses of worship where informality reigns and pastors typically begin a sermon with a clip from a recent movie.

"We are using the iconography of Hollywood to form our vision of the kingdom of God," he said. "We've taken the crosses and other traditional symbols out of the modern church because they make the seeker uncomfortable. Then we replaced them with symbols of the culture. Evangelical Christians have largely given up the symbols of their faith. All the trappings that say this is the home of the body of Christ are gone. People will put something in its place—music, drama—symbols of the culture we bring into the church so we feel comfortable, just as if we were at the mall and the movie theater. We are trying to create a Christian culture using someone else's symbols. It is like using styrofoam plates instead of Mom's china. This is creating a crisis in the inner life of the church."

Currently, Hollywood is open to the supernatural, so he sees no little irony in how some emergent churches have brought liturgical objects back into their worship. "Right now, crosses and candles are icons of our culture," he says. "Once the culture changes, where do those crosses and candles go?" But he wearies of the constant "movements" that sweep the church.

"I and another evangelical pastor sat down and listed eighteen different fads that swept through American churches in the past few decades," he said. "Every time something comes up, people jump on the bandwagon like lemmings. It's trying to find the quick fix that will add to your members: home Bible studies, hanging loose, Jabez, purpose-driven, Toronto blessing—there is this spiritual exhaustion."

So there you have it: several ways that people are trying to reinvent church—or return to its roots—in twenty-first-century America. Before getting too far into why more and more Americans are skipping church, I wanted to point out some good-faith efforts to reverse this trend. Most of the personalities interviewed here had a common theme: that things cannot remain the same old same old. McLaren even created a book, *Everything Must Change*, released in October 2007, that fortunately for him has echoed a major theme of the 2008 election season. It's not news anymore that people are dissatisfied with church as usual. It is news when a pastor can figure out a winning combination in a time when many people are searching for the key.

5

◇◇◇◇◇◇◇◇

THE LONELIEST NUMBER

Why Singles over Thirty-five Are Saying Good-bye

It was the last day of September 2007, a gorgeous early fall morning with blue skies and the leaves on the trees slowly turning orange and yellow. I was seated in a crowded evangelical church. The pastor was preaching on different kinds of love and was getting lots of laughter from the congregation as he read and commented on some of the more erotic passages in the Song of Solomon. It was still a G-rated sermon, but everyone was getting the pastor's point that sex is very important to God.

As the preacher worked toward his conclusion, it grew obvious he felt he had to say something about single people, who—if they are obedient Christians—are not allowed to receive and give erotic love. The tenor of the sermon changed; suddenly there was a mention of Mother Teresa, who "found love in a way that few of us could ever begin to imagine," he said, even though she had to do without sex, children, or a husband. I found this a curious choice, since a new book on the famous nun's years of spiritual dryness and inability to feel God's love had come out just the month before.

"Sex can be wonderful," he continued, "but it's like an ice cream cone or a dish of crème brûlée—fantastic for the moment but then it's gone." What's really important, he reminded his listeners, is intimacy with God. To press home his point that one can be happy while celibate, he cited a vision that one of his single congregants had told him about. She was alone at a crowded train station filled with couples. Then Jesus appeared at her side, took her by the hand, and led her onto the train, at which point all her unhappy thoughts on singleness disappeared.

This pastor was married and had several grown children, all of whom had married young. Photos of this man's extended family were posted on the church bulletin board. Apparently, intimacy with God as one's sole comfort in life would have to do for the many singles in his congregation but not for him or his family.

That afternoon I got a phone call from a fellow single who had also been to that service. "Well," she said, "what did you think about *that*?"

This pastor had been a very well-meaning and kind person in all my encounters with him, but his unwitting assumptions cut to the bone. I was not surprised to learn his large church has no ministry to singles over thirty-five, even though the Washington, D.C., area has one of the country's highest percentages of unmarried people. Checking around with several other churches in the area, I found less than a handful reaching out to singles. It was the custom, I learned, for church leaders to refer the uncoupled to McLean Bible Church, a regional megacongregation with a large singles ministry.

But the bulk of McLean's singles staff reaches out to the three thousand people in its under–thirty-five group, which has its own weekly Sunday service. Far fewer staff and resources are devoted to older singles; which is probably why there's a huge drop in involvement of people in this age group at a church that's considered the Cadillac of singles ministry for the Washington, DC, area.

A staffer told me their 45 and up group draws 130 people, not a huge number, considering this is one of the only ministries to older Christian singles in a metropolitan area of 5 million people. So where have the missing people gone? I'm not convinced they all got married. And did these other churches essentially contract out their singles ministry to McLean because the megachurch offered a specialized ministry not possible for a smaller church? Or did these churches simply not want to deal with these families of one?

Unwanted as singles may be in the church, the rest of the world has caught on to this once-ignored demographic. America's 89.6 million singles head just over half (50.3 percent) of all American households, according to the 2006 census. About 50 million have never married. These are record levels in American society, according to Stephanie Coontz, director of public education for the Council on Contemporary Families in a quote from the *New York Times*. The article, which ran early in 2007, juggled the census figures a bit differently to come up with figures for women. Fifty-one percent of American women are living without a spouse, it said.

Although one-person households have been called the "new nuclear family," these sole proprietors do not necessarily want to stay single. In a February 2006 Pew Research Center poll in which people in forty-five nations were asked what made them happy, 43 percent of married people said they were "very happy," compared to 24 percent of singles.

Statistically, singles lead the pack in terms of people sliding out the back doors of America's churches, and many singles never make it in the front door. In October 2005 University of Virginia scholar Brad Wilcox released some statistics on single men and church. Thirty-two percent of married men attend church weekly, he said. Fifteen percent of single men do. Thirty-nine percent of married women attend church weekly; 23 percent of single women do.

"Twenty-eight percent of the decline in religious attendance over the last thirty years can be attributed to . . . the fact that fewer adults are now married with children," he said. "In a word, changes in family structure have played an important role in the nation's secularization." Unmarried men, he added, tend to be unchurched men. Unmarried, childless men are 57 percent less likely to attend church weekly than married men with children.

And if they do come through the church door, they hear sermons like the one my friend and I heard that September day.

Creating Eunuchs

Ellen Varughese, author of the 1992 book *The Freedom to Marry*, told me she also used to be on the receiving end of sermons about sexual purity. She was not disputing biblical instructions to be chaste, but she did have a problem with the way the message was delivered. At the end of one such talk, her pastor admitted God had given him a wonderful wife, but the singles in his audience had to remain celibate.

"In other words," Varughese said, "God hasn't given us anything. I still cringe. We were never taught that marriage was the Lord's provision for our sexual needs. Oh, we definitely understood that marriage was God's provision for the pastors of this world, that elite group that God gave good things to. But we were never given to understand that we would someday marry. We were consigned to being satisfied, content, and celibate singles."

She came up with a term, *eunuch makers*, based on the term used in Matthew 19:12, to apply to some of the mind games she found in the conservative churches she attended. She relates an encounter she had with a pastor she met in Dallas before she met her husband.

> I asked a singles pastor there what he felt his most important ministry was. He listed several spiritual-sounding things such as helping singles walk more closely with Jesus and teaching them how to live victorious single lives. I asked whether his church had any program for helping singles marry. He gave a slightly horrified look and said, "Why certainly not! We can't allow our singles ministry to degenerate into a matchmaking service."

Then Varughese met a pastor from India who told her that in his country, Christians assume everyone is to be married, unless they have a specific call from God to stay single. Pastors like him, he said, take it on themselves to find Christian mates for the singles in their congregation. She was so impressed with the man that they eventually married.

Indian Christians have gotten it right on this point. Twenty years ago, when I wrote *Purity Makes the Heart Grow Stronger* for singles, it was in an era when the only book available on the topic was Elisabeth Elliot's *Passion and Purity*. Although a noble—and groundbreaking—effort, Elliot was widowed twice and married three times, hardly the experience of most single Christians. For about a year, I was on the singles speaking circuit and was surprised by the reluctance among the various singles leaders I encountered

to help people get married. It seemed as though the purpose for many of their groups was to keep people single,
not to match them up. Some did not want their singles
groups becoming known as meat markets, but I never understood what could be wrong with helping singles meet
each other.

As I collected anecdotes for this chapter, I kept running
into stories about ministers who were indifferent about
singles issues until their own children began looking for
mates. One especially stood out. While hiring three youth
ministry workers, a pastor was refusing requests for at least
a part-time staff member for his rapidly growing singles
ministry. In October 1997 he attended the huge Promise Keepers rally on the Mall in Washington, D.C., where
he found a young man to whom he introduced his oldest daughter. One thing led to another and within a short
time, the two were engaged. The pastor and his wife were
delighted; not only had they landed a Christian son-in-law,
but he was stunningly good-looking to boot. They went
about the church, telling everyone how wonderfully God
had answered their prayers.

The incident caused quite a stir among the single women
in that church. Definitely this pastor was fulfilling a fatherly
duty, but while he feathered his own nest, couldn't he have
expended some of his energy on matching them up? Slowly
the singles group at that church disintegrated as its members
lost heart. So did one at a thriving, racially mixed church in
west Houston, where I interviewed Mary, a single mom who
was steaming over a Father's Day message. The preacher had
suggested a woman's role was to fry the chicken and bake
the pies. It used to be that singles did all the grunt work in
Mary's congregation until they began tending to their own
lives.

"On Mission Monday," she told me, "I have other things to do," such as taking classes for her doctorate. "There is a spiritual uprising going on in church," she said. "We're getting family, family, family from the pulpit. So we're pulling away. We're not finding fulfillment there any longer."

Singles said they shrugged off patronizing attitudes for a time but eventually their patience wore off. "For years I thought I would meet my wife in a church setting," a man from an Arizona megachurch told me. "But I believe the attitudes toward singles that exist in most churches drive singles away. I have recently thrown in the towel and started going back into the secular world to meet women. Sexual temptations are greater and more abundant, but at least I am meeting people."

In addition to the book on purity, I've also written a booklet of Bible studies for singles plus numerous magazine articles. Occasionally people call my office for advice or feedback. One day the woman on the line introduced herself as Debbie Maken. Her family was from Calcutta, and she was a litigation attorney living in Ft. Lauderdale. She was twenty-eight when it dawned on her the teachings at her church actively worked to keep her single. Basically, she said, many churches teach that marriage is a gift that only some fortunate people receive. Marriage will spontaneously happen for some but not for others, and for those who are part of the latter group, they must assume God has called them to singleness by default.

I told her she needed to check out Varughese's book because both women were saying the same thing. For the next two years, we compared notes while she wrote her 2006 book *Getting Serious about Getting Married.*

Churches teach "you must be content with your singleness since you cannot change or control it; Jesus is all you need to be happy," she wrote. "You should be single with great fulfillment, joy, and an absence of loneliness. To be discontent with your single status is sin. God wants you to be single, whether you actually want to be or not."

Maken knew it was time to change her theology as well as her church. She contacted an Indian matchmaking service, found a man from Punjab whom she liked, got married, and now has two daughters. She too believes Christians have a duty to marry, unless God has specifically called them to be single. Drawing from sources ranging from the Bible to the Westminster Catechism, she argues convincingly that deliberately delaying marriage is a sin. I do not have the space to reproduce her entire argument, but her case is compelling: the best way to promote family values is to help those who wish to marry. Churches, she contends, should quit acting as stumbling blocks to the pursuit of marriage.

The Male Viewpoint

Nationally four out of ten adult men are single. Of those four, three have never been married, and one is divorced or separated. Especially for the three who have never been married, church programs on parenting, marriage, and divorce recovery (the typical singles programs that churches have, if they offer any) are meaningless. In 2004 a Barna survey identified the typical unchurched person as a thirty-eight-year-old single male who lives on the West Coast or in the northeastern United States. While 26 percent of America's adults are never-married singles, 37 percent of the unchurched population fits that description.

When casting about for reasons that single men in particular avoid church, I found a volunteer in his early fifties from northern Virginia who wrote an essay, which, with his permission, I am reproducing in part to describe what single men face in churches and why they leave. There are all sorts of admonitions out there in the Christian sub-culture to pray for and protect the family, but here is an example of the battle millions of singles face in even form-ing a family.

He begins with how, in 1979, he told his small group he wanted to get married.

> I was rebuked by the elders because, according to them, the Bible says it is better to be single to serve God better. They, obviously, were married, and I didn't understand, if they felt so strongly about being single, why they themselves weren't single. When I would ask for prayer, I would get a lecture about being content, and was told I needed to stop focusing on self and serve God better.

Fast-forward to 1982, when he turned twenty-seven.

> I went to the prayer rail several times seeking God's wisdom on marriage. I was told by the pastor that maybe God wanted me to be single, and that there wasn't much I could do about the situation, other than accept my circumstances. I was told that, if God wanted me to have a relationship with a woman, he would bring this person into my life.
>
> The pastor also preached a sermon on singleness, saying that if a person was over forty and no one had come into his or her life, then this was God's calling of celibacy.

My friend switched churches and began to seek counsel of his new pastors.

> The first minister I talked to told me that God's plan for my life could be to be single, and I just needed to accept

this. Several years later, I went for advice to another pastor, who chewed me out in front of several friends for not being open to celibacy. Later, I wrote him again asking for advice, and he wrote back, "Perhaps being single is your vocation." I went to the senior pastor and he shrugged his shoulders and said it was too bad, but God doesn't promise everyone a mate.

I was involved in a men's accountability group with two married men. I expressed my desire to marry. The head of this group said he could not pray for a wife for me, because he wasn't convinced that I should be married. I was eventually confronted by two leaders of this group and told that I was immediately to stop this "whining" about wanting to be married. When I again raised this issue several years later, I was told by the leader of the group that he would no longer pray with me and that I was out of the group. He compared my desire to marry with "a black man who was constantly whining to God about being black and wanting to be white."

By this time, it was the mid-1990s. My friend joined a dating service that went bankrupt a month after he joined. The head of his church's prayer ministry said God allowed this to show him he didn't need the dating service. My friend even talked to a bishop in our denomination who suggested he join a monastery. Another singles minister told him his singleness was a call from God because if God had not sent him anyone by this time (he was in his forties), the answer was no. Naturally, he left the church.

"I want to make it very clear that I am not bitter," he said, "but I have lost interest in the church and have to whip myself to go and make myself serve."

The reason singles like this man are treated in such a demeaning fashion is a puzzle. People living alone are one of America's fastest-growing groups. Do churches constantly use the mantra "family friendly" to describe themselves, build "family life centers" alongside the sanctuary, and fill the typical Sunday bulletin with activities for the family because they wish the intact family were a reality for the majority of Americans? Or do they think that somehow, by emphasizing the family, they can lower the divorce rate or the number of home-alone kids? That may explain why, at Holy Communion, some churches have instituted the custom of families receiving the bread and wine together. But what kind of message does that send to the single person who gets to stand before the altar rail alone?

According to census data released in 2005, only 23.7 percent of all American households are married couples with children. "Faith and Family in America," a 2005 analysis by University of Akron sociologist John C. Green, says only 18.5 percent of all families meet the traditional nuclear family ideal: married, never divorced, with children at home. The largest demographic (25.6 percent) is childless couples. Church leaders uphold the former model as the ideal Christian family, but the statistics indicate they are chasing the wind. In some denominations, such as the Episcopal Church, fully half of the members are single.

The flip side of the coin is that churches pay attention to singles only in terms of how they can serve. In interview after interview I've heard from singles who were asked to volunteer for the mission field, teach Sunday school, fill in at the nursery, and other activities supporting the rearing of Christian youth. They are often expected to attend to the priorities of the married, while the married rarely think about—much less act on—the priorities of singles, such as having a place to go for the holidays or being introduced to eligible mates so they can start their own family. I heard of one small group at a Virginia church that took on the duty of praying specifically for its singles that they would marry. Within a year, the level of marriages in that group had skyrocketed. Then the group stopped praying and the level began to drop. This brings up an interesting thought: if prayer helps singles find mates, then is there an opposite force out there working at keeping them alone?

And if the family is under attack in today's America—and there are plenty of interest groups saying this is the case—is there a similar spiritual attack against those who wish to form families? Whatever the metaphysical realities are, singles are wising up—and opting out. They have had it with putting in twenty or more years of service to their churches and getting little or nothing back.

"We are not the church's easy free labor pool to do the undesirable jobs no one else wants to do in the name of 'servanthood,' 'contentment,' and 'humility,'" wrote "Richard," a man who had seen one of my online essays on singleness. "We are anointed individuals like our married counterparts with unique spiritual giftings and callings that others need in their lives."

Married versus Single

Much of the problem for singles is the lack of Christian men, which has been at crisis levels for a long time. Alveda King, niece of Martin Luther King, addresses some of these issues in her 2001 book *I Don't Want Your Man, I Want My Own*, about the very real shortage of men facing black Christian women. Their married "sisters," anxious to hold onto their men, are hostile. King suggests that married Christian women should pray for their single sisters instead of treating them with suspicion or hatred. "It is cruel and hypocritical to expect women not to have needs just because they do not have husbands," she writes.

Then she adds:

> It is condescending for a woman who has a husband, whose emotional, sexual, and other needs are met, to look down upon and judge single women who are struggling with desires to have those needs met. A woman's sexual and emotional desires do not diminish just because she finds herself unmarried. If she has been married, and these needs have been met, the woman is in for some very serious challenges and needs support and prayer to overcome temptation.

There are solutions to this problem, one of which is bringing up and dealing with sexual issues. Back in the 1990s, when I was doing a lot more writing on this topic, I found two surveys—one from the singles group at Peachtree Presbyterian Church in Atlanta and the other a survey of single Southern Baptists. Both revealed that only one-third of the respondents had abstained from sex. For their 1991 book, *Single Adult Passages: Uncharted Territories*, Carolyn Koons and Michael Anthony had surveyed 1,500 single Christians, most of whom attended church at least once a week. They found significant levels of sexual activity.

Of the women surveyed, 39 percent were virgins, 27 percent had had four or more sexual partners, 22 percent had lived with a man, 5 percent had had more than twenty sexual partners, and 14 percent had had sex within the past six months. Of the men, 33 percent were virgins, 35 percent had had four or more sexual partners, 22 percent had lived with a woman, 10 percent had had more than twenty sexual partners, and 23 percent had had sex within the past six months. These figures show a much higher chastity level than what's out there in the secular world. The Alan Guttmacher Institute, a sexual health statistics group, said in

2006 that "most" (at least 70 percent) of all teens have had sex by age nineteen.

An intriguing subgroup is the one-third of both men and women who have kept their virginity. Judging by the people with whom I have corresponded or whom I have interviewed over a twenty-year period (the *Purity* book came out in 1988), their Christianity is the only thing keeping them out of someone else's bed. Many would do anything for some support. They don't dare admit their sexual inexperience at the office. The culture tells them they have missed out on life's greatest experience, while at the same time at church, not one word of encouragement comes from the pulpit or even their friends.

"Richard" wrote me: "I, being an almost thirty-four-year-old Christian single (never-married) male, have felt the alienation and isolation that Christian singles face. Singles are seen as dysfunctional people with problems, sex-crazed animals with hormones out of control, and people who do not put a whole lot of money in the plate. Single men in their thirties are seen as gay or in my case, the 'techno geek nerd,' and single women in their thirties are seen as crabby old maids. . . . I am single, not shingles."

His conclusion: "I too am a committed evangelical Christian man in his thirties who has had it with their family-centric churches and quietly slipped out."

"It takes an extraordinarily brave person to live this lifestyle," said "Ray," a man from Alabama with normal appetites who has stayed a virgin into his forties. He is one of a very rare breed who is called to singleness. Referring to Revelation 14:3–4, "I believe we will have a special role and status in heaven, that there is something very mystical about virginity that can only be fully understood when we get there."

He had responded to one of my books, hoping to find someone who understood people like him. Ray is part of a subculture I never heard talked about among church leaders, as the bulk of admonishment and counseling seems geared toward the two-thirds of a typical singles group that is sexually active. Depressed by this quintuple loss: no children, no soul mate, no legal sex, no social standing as a couple, and of course no wedding day, the faithful slip away.

"As a lifelong church attendee, leaving the body of Christ was not easy," a female college professor wrote me. "As a now forty-something single, feeling like a leftover and a failure for not attaining the Christian mandate to marry and procreate, well, I just couldn't take it anymore. At times, my loneliness makes me long for the release of suicide. At church, the loneliness was most unbearable. I still often wonder what hidden sin that I have committed to be denied a family."

Some married people get impatient with singles, saying it's not hard to find a mate these days with the Internet. I talked with "Karen," a female journalist in Washington in her forties, who has long prayed for a mate. Karen wields enormous influence in her job, but she's had no luck in finding a husband.

"I know my job is sapping all my extra energy and time," she said, "but what am I supposed to do: take a nine-dollar-an-hour job at a grocery store so I can go husband hunting? I don't have time for my girlfriends, much less for finding a guy."

She had tried a supposedly Christian Internet matchmaking service only to find herself paired with men with whom she had nothing in common. The fact that these men stated in their profiles they wanted women with sexual experience was a huge turnoff. After a year, she called it quits.

On a personal level, I have not experimented much with online dating services, as my experience with them has been negative. Other acquaintances have done far more work along this line. A handful have struck gold. Everyone else has come up empty.

Matchmaker, Matchmaker

Some singles have decided not to wait for their churches to come help them find mates. They have taken matters into their own hands and gone in directions most pastors I know are afraid to even discuss. In the summer of 2007, I got an email from a single, never-married man in Chicago who was telling me about the singles scene in that city. Then he mentioned one woman—who attended a church we both knew of—who had arranged to be inseminated with donated egg and sperm to have her own child. She was so pleased with the result, she underwent the procedure a second time.

"This certainly says something about our society and our churches," my correspondent mused. "We have not succeeded in making Christian dating and marrying into something simple, so now we have the reverse. Getting married now seems like rocket science—at least for those who have not figured it out yet, myself included—and the 'rocket science' of in vitro fertilization seems comparatively simple, as long as one can afford it."

The future is here. By the time I had been in the Washington area a few years, it was clear there were too few men available for the many professional women in town. I joined a New York–based group, Single Mothers by Choice (SMC), to look into the possibility of becoming a mother if not a wife. I chose adoption as my path, but I was in the minority. Most of the women were inseminating themselves, as it was far cheaper than adoption, and they wanted to experience pregnancy.

Many of the comments on SMC's Listserve and in their newsletters were from women who said they were Jewish and they were doing this with the support of their families. Having a family is important in their culture, no matter how one does it. Of course getting a mate first is preferable: Orthodox Rabbi Schmuley Boteach, in his 1999 book *Dating Secrets of the Ten Commandments*, says God has a stake in marriage. "According to Jewish thought," he writes, "the Almighty has a soul mate intended for each and every one of us."

While I was a reporter for the *Houston Chronicle*, I did a piece on how the local Jewish Community Center (JCC) had started up a matchmaking service. Even though Houston was filled with huge churches, none of them had anything like it.

But at the JCC, it was not a shameful thing to admit the need for help in finding a mate. For thousands of years, parents have done the marriage arranging. Only in the past century have singles been left on their own with no help from their family. Courtship—where the parents are very involved—has come back into vogue in some Christian circles, but only among twenty-somethings. The over-thirty set is more reluctant to involve their parents, as they have a clearer idea of what they are looking for. A matchmaker is more dispassionate than a family member. Jews assume that everyone needs to marry; it's just a matter of finding the right person. The JCC in Houston employed several women to assemble photos in scrapbooks and—for a fee—interview singles with the hope of making a match.

Christians, I realized, think that marriage will just happen, but Jews understand the need for some human intervention. That is why their tradition allows for a matchmaker—like the character Yente in *Fiddler on the Roof*—to help things along.

What if churches had matchmakers? If singles tell most pastors of their wish to marry, they will likely get a puzzled look and a suggestion to trust God's sovereignty, while the typical rabbi will help them pair up.

Singles desperately want to marry, although many feel ashamed to admit it. If churches automatically assisted their singles in finding mates—unless specifically told not to—this would remove the shame factor and restore the marriage process as a natural stage in life. It would also be easier to find theologically compatible mates this way. Plus, a ministry along these lines would relieve the pastors, who often have been unwilling to help.

Singles are immensely valuable to the church; after all, Jesus was single. But would he approve of how so many churches have become singles warehouses instead of wedding makers?

6

◇◇◇◇◇◇◇◇

NOT SO SOLID TEACHING

Why Christians Cannot Exit the Obstetrics Ward

It was a chilly Sunday morning in downtown Kansas City, but Bartle Hall, a large gathering place within the city's conference complex, was rocking.

I was watching three thousand people at a "harp and bowl" worship conference sponsored by the International House of Prayer, a twenty-four-hour prayer ministry based in a nearby suburb. The ministry was begun by Mike Bickle, one of the best teachers on the "prophetic" circuit of charismatic Christianity. How Bickle founded Metro Christian Fellowship in Kansas City, then left to devote his time to a prayer project on the city's outskirts is too long a story to tell here, but I had heard a lot about IHOP. I arranged to fly to Kansas City with a photographer to look into the ministry and attend the conference.

After a dazzling ninety minutes of worship, Bickle preached. Instead of lecturing the crowd, he was lamenting the lack of decent content from the pulpit. "The church is suffering from spiritual boredom," he said. "There's tons of babbling in the church, and it really creates a disdain for the preachers."

Clergy who "started out fearless," he added, became timid because now "they have too many people they must keep happy." Then, looking out over the crowd of mostly laity, he added, "Your life is a rebuke to them because they cannot afford to be fearless anymore. Fearless people unsettle and unnerve the structure."

The heart of the pastor—and the centerpiece of most Protestant services—is the sermon. Pastors generally think their sheep are getting a good meal; however, their listeners disagree, according to research by George Barna. In 1993 he found that while only 44 percent of congregations polled rated the preaching they got as excellent, 81 percent of the pastors did so. (An updated 2006 poll of his revealed 98 percent of pastors polled considered themselves effective Bible teachers.)

"Both clergy and laity have recognized for several decades a decline in effective preaching," writes retired University of Texas English professor Elizabeth J. Morgan, whose doctorate was on sermon rhetoric. "The complaints range from dissatisfaction to downright scorn and boycott."

Pastors, she added, "snap a microphone to their lapels and pace back and forth like nervous sheep dogs." Whereas some dress in white suits, others dress ultracasually; a trend she disparaged. "It is the informal style in both looks and words which conceives of sermons as friendly conversations with the man on the street," she added. "But alas, as Englishman A. G. Moore said, 'It is a priest's duty to feed the sheep rather than amuse the goats.'"

The Soul and Passions of a Teacher

People never tell me mediocre teaching is the foremost reason for their leaving a church, but it is a huge factor. Searching for some reasons for why teaching is often substandard, I looked up two people. One was Haddon Robinson, president of Gordon-Conwell Theological Seminary in Massachusetts, a campus of two thousand students. Robinson is a man who in 1996 was named in a Baylor University poll as one of the twelve most effective preachers in the English-speaking world. A decent sermon, he told me, takes twelve to fifteen hours of preparation. Many pastors, he added, are lucky if they get four hours on a Saturday night.

"Study is tough work," he said. "It is easy to be lured away from your desk—by good things. But to preach, you've got to make that high priority. Even as a president of a seminary, I fight for time. I get up at 5 a.m. and I can usually go to bed at 9:30." Moreover, he has to provide content for his 250 radio programs a year, each lasting 15 minutes. "I really have to struggle to get the time to prepare those," he added.

Desperate to cut corners, pastors will download material off the Internet, such as the free sermons at www.pastors.com, the website of Saddleback Church pastor Rick Warren. Robinson said he understands the reasons time-strapped pastors use this resource, but he advises against making it a habit.

"It's a national problem," he said. "If you do this regularly, your brain shrivels up."

I also talked with Patrick Reardon, a professor from my seminary days in Ambridge, Pennsylvania, who left the Episcopal priesthood to become an Orthodox cleric. He loves to teach anything and everything about the Scriptures and the early church fathers and still posts daily Bible devotionals on the website of the Chicago-based *Touchstone* magazine.

Pastors, he told me, are "intellectually lazy. The average evangelical pastor is not a man of the Scriptures," he said. "In fact they are very weak on the Scriptures in the evangelical church. How often are the Scriptures read? How often do the Scriptures form the base of their hymnography?

"They are more into marketing modes for growth, but growth for growth's sake is the philosophy of the cancer cell."

He especially took issue with Willow Creek Community Church, a megachurch in the Chicago area that he faulted for lack of substance and that he called "the apex of marketing of American life. We have some refugees from there. After awhile, you cannot survive on that sort of thing. The people who come here are seriously famished. They have not had a serious meal in years."

In mid-2007 Willow Creek produced a poll of its longtime members that supported Reardon's complaint—to the shock of some on Willow Creek's staff. I will describe this poll in a later chapter, but Reardon had a point. Having studied patristics under him, I knew that my friend makes his congregants do serious work on Sunday mornings. He preaches a half hour on Sundays, which is lengthy for Orthodox priests. Students from Wheaton, Trinity Evangelical, Judson College, and Moody Bible Institute attend. While his All Saints Antiochan Church at Pulaski and Addison streets in west Chicago has grown to more than 150 people, it has several times peeled off some members to help out a struggling parish or to go on an overseas mission. All Saints won't make the cover of *Christianity Today*, but Reardon prides himself on knowing his flock, many of whom have eaten a Sunday meal in his home.

"I have to know everyone in my church by name and have enough affection in my heart that everyone feels loved," he said. "I sincerely like people. I really do."

And at age seventy, he's still going strong.

I decided to look up another person who lived and breathed teaching. In Oregon during the late 1970s and early 1980s, crowds of people were listening to Bettie Mitchell, a local junior high school teacher conducting Bible classes at Portland Community College. Bettie Mitchell's classes were like none I'd heard before on the Bible. She had a way of asking disturbing questions about Jesus's radical demands and playing off our answers to create more questions. Instead of blithely sailing through a passage, she wanted us to interact with it and apply it.

What motivated her was a 1976 trip to Iraq to tour biblical sites. When she climbed the twelve-kilometer-long walls of Nineveh, across the Tigris River from modern-day Mosul, she saw children running atop the wall with their schoolbooks in plastic bags. They were laughing, and it was there, she remembers, God suddenly asked her to take a second look.

"Here are the children," he told her, "but where are the teachers?"

She had no answer.

"I want you to go home and quit your teaching job and teach nothing but my kingdom," he continued.

"My husband will never agree," Mitchell said.

"I will take care of him," he told her.

"All right," she responded, "I will do it."

A few days later in Erbil, a Kurdish city about an hour's drive south of Nineveh, she spotted a little girl with a paper bag, searching for things of value lying on the ground. God spoke again.

"People are like this little girl," he said. "They are looking for something worth saving, but they no longer know what's important and what's worth saving."

Mitchell realized that in much of her teaching up until then, her students had never understood the main point of her lessons. Faced with a challenge to rethink how she was teaching Scripture, she quit her junior high job and began counseling people in her home. The best teaching, she realized, creates maximum impact at the individual level.

"People are sick, mentally ill, furious, and angry with life," she told me. "If the church wants to meet people's needs, it needs to find a way of teaching people so they really get the lesson and know what they are supposed to do with it and how it will change their lives."

Her efforts culminated in the founding of Good Samaritan Ministries in nearby Beaverton. In thirty years it has become a major aid organization benefiting Third World believers and a teaching, healing, and training center for Christian counselors. Mitchell could not find a church that was willing to invest the resources needed to produce good teachers, so she grew them herself. She also learned that people respond best to dialogue-style teaching—or preaching—rather than to a lecture format.

"Straight preaching no longer works with the public, as we no longer learn that way," she now says. "The masses are better educated and no longer so naive to think this one person has all the knowledge and wants to feed it into us. We want to interact with the information. Pastors never connect with their people. They never say, 'What kind of sermon do you need to hear this week?' A good teacher will know every child and will know what motivates every child in his or her classroom. A good teacher makes sure no child fails."

Sliding out of Church

"A lot of teaching does not take into account the sophistication of our listeners," emergent church pastor Brian McLaren told me in an interview. In the past, people have supplemented through extra reading what they are not getting at church. In terms of Bible studies, there does seem to be a dearth of intellectually challenging ones on the market. Scripture Union's *Encounter with God* is widely distributed in churches, but its authors take up too much valuable space citing their sources. The quality of its teachers also varies widely. William Barclay's topical studies and expositions on books of the Bible are much better, but those often can't be found in a typical bookstore. Short of being a seminary student (the one period in my life when I got exceptionally good teaching), I have found little out there besides devotionals and introductory studies.

People who are not learning new insights at church will go shopping elsewhere. Church leaders might learn something from Mormons on this score. The Mormons have an amazing system of early-morning seminars—called "seminary"—for their high-school-age members. Several years in a row, teenagers meet at 6 a.m. to study the tenets of the faith. I did a story on this while a reporter in Houston and had to show up, groggily, at the crack of dawn at a local stake (congregation) where, sure enough, the teens were studying away. This had a major effect in terms of retaining young Mormons.

While your typical evangelical teenager can probably barely explain the basics of the faith, their Mormon counterparts are studying the Scriptures and the Book of Mormon every morning for several years to prep themselves for mission trips. Small wonder this is a fast-growing religion.

In the summer of 2006, Brad Waggoner, president of Lifeway Christian Resources, assigned researchers to ask 469 adults why they had left church. Baptisms were down in the Southern Baptist Convention (SBC), growth was flat, and, according to Gallup, the number of Americans who identified themselves as Southern Baptists had declined from 10 percent in 1995 to 6 percent in 2001. Lifeway wanted to know why.

Many of the reasons people gave seemed lightweight. A few cited hectic schedules and family responsibilities at home. Whereas Sunday used to be a protected day for Sabbath rest, now it was the "new Saturday," with enticements to play sports, watch TV, and shop.

Other responses provided Waggoner more profound reasons for the exodus. Many churches, he found, have done a poor job of grounding people in their faith and laying down what commitment as a Christian means. The typical church was not educating people by teaching Scripture in an understandable and applicable way.

As a result, people slid easily in and out of attendance. Instead of lowering the bar, the church, he concluded, needs to raise it by demanding more, not less. If Orthodox Jews can require all their practitioners to be at home Friday nights for a Sabbath meal, if the Seventh-day Adventists can mandate Saturdays as a day of worship instead of Sundays, if the Mormons can order Monday evening "family nights" among their followers, surely Baptists could raise their standards.

"What's offered in church is just getting dumbed down more and more," reported Chuck Colson in a 2006 *Christianity Today* column. Upset that several Christian radio stations around the country had dropped his and other teaching programs, he found out these same radio stations were filling the empty spots with music. As one station manager told him, "We don't want to do anything that will upset our listeners."

"Evangelicals are in danger of amusing ourselves to death, to borrow the title of the classic Neil Postman book," Colson wrote. "Music is important in the life of the church and can inspire us to focus on Christ. But it cannot take the place of solid teaching."

The situation is a Catch-22; radio stations perceive their listeners are tuning out intellectually challenging material, so they substitute pablum for substance, causing more people to head for the off switch. And at the local church, many believers say they are appalled at what's on the menu and believe they can do better by getting material through books or off the Internet. Richard Kim, an Episcopal-turned-Anglican priest in Detroit, put it succinctly in an email to me: the church is irrelevant, boring, and powerless.

"The Gospel is not preached," he wrote, "or, where it is preached, it is usually in philosophical bla-bla language void of the power of God."

Some have fled to older Christian denominations, as did Ella Moravec, one of my seminary classmates from Pittsburgh. She converted to Orthodoxy in 1997. The rigors of a typical Orthodox year—a rule of prayer, four major periods of fasting each year, the long services, the prostrations in front of the altar, the relics and icons—all have aided in the growth of her spirit in a way many years of evangelicalism did not.

"There's no training in sanctification," she says of her past church life in an evangelical Episcopal congregation. "If you compare the church to a spiritual hospital, all evangelicals have is the obstetrics ward."

Out the Back Door

Although the seeker-friendly movement has brought some new blood into churches, it appears to have done so at the expense of more mature Christians who have bolted after listening to preaching without content and sitting in rushed services that are crammed into less than ninety minutes. Many churches' tendency to win people to Christ, then do nothing for their formation beyond a Christian basics class such as the Alpha program, has sent hordes racing out the back doors.

Evangelist David Wilkerson has long been concerned with the quality of teaching. While going over biblical warnings of terrors leading up to the end times, he thinks—with the perspective of a resident of a city that got the brunt of the September 11, 2001, terrorist attacks—that more attacks are in store for Americans. Both secular and Christian sources are warning of perilous times ahead, but "How is the body of Christ responding to these warnings?" he asked in his February 5, 2007, newsletter.

"In many churches, there is no mention of atrocities, of terrorism, of tragic pandemics," he wrote. "Instead, the messages being brought forth from those pulpits are comprised of motivational pep talks, jokes, entertainment. It's all spiritual baby food, with no word spoken about coming judgments. Yet the handwriting is on the wall, declared by Scripture and echoed by the world: a dreadful day is ahead."

In another newsletter the month before, he rued that repentance—a major part of Christian conversion as shown in Acts 2—simply isn't taught in church. Are pastors "afraid of losing people?" he wrote. "Do they fear being unable to make mortgage payments? Are they mindful of needing people to give more toward the church's growing expenses? I'm convinced these things combine to persuade good men to preach a soft message. . . . I'm certain God is grieved over churches that reject his message of repentance. In fact, it is my belief that the Holy Spirit will not abide in such churches."

In fairness to those who teach, part of the problem is believers who are too jaundiced to ingest spiritual meat, according to Pam and Dick Ewing, who are former church planters.

Twenty years ago, they moved from Portland to Washington State's Methow Valley just east of the magnificent Cascade Mountains and not far from the Canadian border. They built their own log cabin home near the gentle foothills and purple peaks to the west of Winthrop, a town of sixty-five hundred. While working by day as a cross-country ski instructor and furniture maker, Dick used his free time to disciple Christian men. Their vision was to develop a Christian retreat along the lines of the Swiss community L'Abri. The Ewings liked the idea of having people live either with them or near them and learn the essence of Christianity.

Within a few years, that vision had gone sour. There were a lot of evangelical Christians in that corner of the state, but the local churches were involved in endless turf wars. The Ewings got involved in a few, even though that was the last thing they wanted. The churches that survived seemed fixated on the basics.

"There's no place for me with my background and skills," said Dick sadly, referring to his years in seminary and as a pastor. "It's almost an imposition on people for me to teach." Three men from his seminary were in the area, he said. One was a pastor, but Dick and the other man had dropped out of church altogether.

"I think the problem is when you know too much," Pam said. "You have nowhere to share your insights, or you see through the shallowness and don't want to deal with it."

After years of discipling Christians around the Pacific Northwest, this couple seemed to understand the mind-set of the typical evangelical. Most, they said, did not know how to study their Bibles, much less develop a coherent Christian worldview or defend their faith. Thus the large, badly taught evangelical multitudes have minimal effect on their culture.

"There is little or no teaching on how to die to ourselves and what that may look like," Pam said. "Nor are we taught how to live by faith and what that looks like, what Paul writes about in 2 Corinthians 2:14–6:13. Therefore, we are missing the power of the Holy Spirit to see miracles in changed lives, our own as well as others. That's where the dissatisfaction comes from.

"The Holy Spirit, through our consciences, tells us that there is much more to the Christian life than we are experiencing, but we do not know how to find it or what it looks like. Instead, we tend to seek fulfillment in the things that are seen instead of the unseen, but they never satisfy."

It's no small thing that teachers such as the Ewings are walking away from two thousand years of advice from apostles, martyrs, reformers, and saints who all say that participation in church matters. They and other mature believers were not seeing any spiritual development from their church involvements; if anything, they were losing ground and getting vilified in the process. To them, there was more spiritual danger in staying in church than going it alone. Leaving church is a last, desperate resort for people who should be leaders in the body of Christ, but increasing numbers of people are leaving.

But is anyone listening? In mid-2007, I ordered the first part of *Church Outside the Walls*, a video produced by the California-based Family Room Media. The first part, "The Drop-Outs," contained interviews with several folks who weren't in church and were loving it. Church to them had become somewhat like the movie *The Matrix*, about millions of people blissfully living their lives as part of a computer-generated fantasy, whereas in reality they were slaves hooked up to machines. The church, the video suggested, is similar, involved in its own little world, completely separate from the raw realities of life.

"Why would I want to bring anyone here?" said one of the men interviewed for the video. "This is not how I function at home or at work. At church you don't even talk the same. It has become more and more a realization of performance burnout."

All the "dropouts" in the video said church was mainly gatherings and programs but not a strengthener of their relationship with God. David Frederickson, the narrator for the film, said many people who leave are tired of the never-ending religious obligations.

"Church is too patterned after corporate America," he said. "Church is a business and the congregation is its customers."

What's Lacking in Church Teachings

When syndicated columnist Mike McManus experienced a recovery from a near-divorce, he began wondering why he never heard anything in church about how to solve marital problems. He and his wife founded their own ministry, Marriage Savers, to help floundering couples who, like them, were not getting any help. As his ministry grew, he realized no one preached on related issues, such as cohabitation and sex outside of marriage, even though congregants were struggling with these matters in their private lives. Despite his myriad columns on the topic—plus the contributions of many other authors—by early 2007, not much had changed.

"They're not preaching on real issues—divorce, chastity, cohabitation—that people are facing," McManus told me. "We hear another sermon on Abraham; who cares about that? There's an avoidance of the big issues people are facing." Adding a statistic from a 1991 Focus on the Family survey of five thousand pastors and their spouses that found more than 50 percent of all pastors' wives polled listed themselves as "severely depressed," he guessed the issue strikes a bit too close to home for many clergy.

"The church is a big zero when it comes to marriage," he added. "They don't know what works because seminaries aren't teaching anything about it."

Even the black church, renowned for the preaching excellence of many of its pastors, is falling down on the marriage issue, wrote Sherman Haywood Cox II, author of the book *You Can Preach*. In a September 1, 2007, post on his www .soulpreaching.com site, he mourned that so few preachers were speaking out about domestic violence, even after a Georgia preacher, Bishop Thomas Weeks, was charged with assault after beating up his wife, evangelist Juanita Bynum, in an Atlanta parking lot. She quickly filed for divorce.

Cox wrote:

> I love black preaching. I love the style that African American preachers use in bringing a word from God. However, African American preaching is more than whooping, shouting and style. It is also a prophetic engagement with the powers that be. It stands up against wickedness in all places even if that wickedness finds itself in our midst.

Teaching on unanswered prayer is another huge hole in the preaching syllabus. Judging by the excellent sales of Henry Blackaby's 1998 book *Experiencing God*, people want to connect with the Almighty, but they flounder on the shoals of unanswered prayer and failure to get through to a heavenly throne room. Or, if they are sick, the healing miracles of the New Testament act more as a rebuke than a comfort.

In various interviews, I learned how stories of God's power contrast painfully with what believers are experiencing on the ground today. After a while, frustrated churchgoers concluded either something got mixed up in the translation or they simply don't cut it as Christians and they might as well bow out now. For preachers not to admit the disconnect is to perpetuate the aura of unreality in today's church.

David Frederickson is a Sacramento-area pastor whose 2006 book *When the Church Leaves the Building* comes packaged with the aforementioned *Church Outside the Walls* video. He says self-doubt is the rule, not the exception, with Christians.

"People think, *Is it only me who's like this? Everyone else seems so happy*," he told me. "People feel isolated, especially if there are these victorious testimonies. People feel there is something wrong with them."

Frederickson has been through several church experiments and found the antidote to this feeling of self-doubt is smaller home group–style churches that get people to reconnect with God. If people feel as though their presence matters at church, then they may realize their presence matters to God. They also find out their doubts are not unusual.

"There is a great lack of authentic relationships and no community in church," he said. "In an institution, everywhere is hush-hush and if something goes wrong, people are stunned. In a typical church, there are so few relationships.

"But when you develop relationships, you find you are not the only one. When people do know each other, they are honest and transparent. I say we have to have genuine relationship before we even start having church meetings."

A related reason for the exodus from churches is the lack of teaching beyond the basics. Chris Jackson, thirty-six, senior pastor of Grace Church of La Verne in La Verne, California—and author of the 2007 book *Loving God When*

You Don't Love the Church, says people are not taught how to endure through the long haul.

"I am running into a lot of people who are disillusioned," he told me. "They have paid their dues, done all the meetings, done all the involvement, and that is not bringing the life change they thought it would.

"And we have had elders leave the church, some of our most precious people. They didn't leave mad; they left burned out. The hunger in people today is for a combination of practical truth they can apply and experience. People are looking for Jesus, period. If they found a place they felt embodied a relationship with him, far fewer people would leave the church. We weren't created for programs or activities."

His first daughter, who was born brain-damaged, died at the age of three. He said, "We heard every Christian cliché, every pat answer. That made me want to wrestle with the big issues, the big questions. We take those biblical promises and misapply them and make the truth of Scripture almost seem like a joke. People try too hard to give the right answer and be religious. I do not think there is often a platform for real honesty. And if things go badly, people are told they do not have enough faith; they are not praying hard enough."

Most people don't like to fail, so when they get enlisted into a faith in which they cannot hear the Lord's simplest directions or get their prayers answered, they check out fast. Most either slide into a costless Christianity that's easily maintained or simply give up.

7

<small>◇◇◇◇◇◇◇◇</small>

IS THE PASTOR THE PROBLEM?

Or Is the Whole System Broken?

Raised Lutheran, Dan Bailey was a missiology graduate from Columbia International University in South Carolina, holder of a master's degree in divinity from Trinity Evangelical Divinity School in Deerfield, Illinois, and a Reformed pastor. "I was *the* evangelist in high school," he recalls. "I was totally on fire for Christ; I smoked pot in grade school and became a Christian in high school. I had one Bible study only for people who had smoked marijuana and had another for jocks."

Although he'd planned to be a missionary, he got sidetracked into a youth pastorate, was ordained in the Reformed Church in America, settled in western Michigan, and lasted twenty years as a pastor.

"I was thoroughly evangelical," he said, "but the Reformed movement destroyed me." He was referring to churches based on Calvinism, a Protestant theology originating in Europe in the fifteenth century. Calvinism has distinctive doctrines on grace, salvation, and God's sovereignty. It was not burnout or sexual problems that caused a ruckus in his church. It was jazz music. When he began taking it up as a hobby, his congregation disapproved.

"Everyone wants their pastor to be real," he said. "Really? What happens when he really is? I began to see first I am a human being and then a pastor. I couldn't be myself. People had too many cultural and role expectations. Plus, parts of me were changing that just don't fit the church anymore."

He began wondering about certain areas of theology and morality he had always taken for granted. For instance, he said, "Evangelicals believe in the inerrancy of Scripture, but you look at the Old Testament and there's genocide there. I always wondered why Jews worry about anti-Semitism when they committed genocide at the orders of their God—killing men, women, children, even their animals? My tradition never allowed me to question that."

He began to rethink his views on homosexuality but knew well enough to keep those thoughts to himself. He began to wonder if he had outgrown Christianity, if that was possible.

"When I was at a party, could I speak openly about what I thought? No. You can't even begin to express your thoughts as a minister. I was forty-five years old; I could not think the way I wanted to think; my marriage was not my marriage; my children were not my children; everything was always being explored by other people. The gospel you've given to others is not given back to you. "

He began to admit he didn't have answers to the many questions people were raising, and no one he knew had answers. His faith seemed to have no final answers. It was more like an onion; the deeper he went, the more layers there were. The first thing he let go was his literal take on the Bible.

"When you do not have to defend the Book anymore, you allow yourself to be free a little bit," he said. "You can say this began as a tribalistic religion that the prophets expanded a little bit. I began to teach and preach in a much more open way. September 11 also taught me as a minister I am very accountable. Those hate ideas came from those men's theologies. The attitudes I teach from my pulpit get translated. I began teaching about tolerance more."

Then, "There were some wolf packs after me," he said. "Not one, not two, but three powerful people in a church, they can take you down. They don't get their way, so they go after and after you. Finally ministers leave because they are so tired. They just cannot fight it anymore. People are so mean in church and relentless in attacking their pastors. A lot of time they do not believe in reconciliation; they just want to destroy you. I can see why the effective ministers are the distant ones, the political ones, the ones good at playing chess. But that's not me. I let my soul out, and they attacked that. I left the church because I outgrew it. I left it because of a midlife crisis and I didn't want to be a pastor for the next twenty-five years. And I left it because the values of the gospel could not be lived out there."

Having quit church in October 2006, Bailey is a nursing student. When I asked him where he was in terms of being a Christian, he couldn't say. "The things I know to be true, I know more deeply now," he finally said. "I think people in a crisis with church need to zero-program their life, get down to the basics, then rebuild from there. Get out of all the roles you played: pastor, believer, and so on. What remains is Christ's suffering and beauty. Because suffering is part of life, and if God was not willing to suffer, then he isn't part of our life."

No one in the American church is more fragile—or bears the brunt of more frustration—than the pastor. Laity are unhappy with their leaders, and their leaders are leaving in droves. According to a 1998 Pew Foundation study, half of all ordained ministers quit within their first five years, often because of burnout.

Needing a Stopping Place

In mid-2006 I interviewed Barbara Brown Taylor, an Episcopal priest and author of *Leaving Church*, her story of pastoring a congregation in rural northeast (Habersham County) Georgia. The cover of her book showed a white dove just released from a cage.

Describing herself as "an introvert and a perfectionist," she told me that her idea of the perfect job became a clergy grinder. "As I aged, there became a friction between my role and soul, which I simply needed to address," she said. "I needed a job with a stopping place."

One key problem was the unanswered prayers of her flock.

"On my worst nights, I lay in bed feeling like a single parent unable to sleep because I knew I did not have enough love in me to go around," she wrote.

> God was the boundless lover, but for many people, God was the parent who had left. They still read about him in the Bible and sang about him in hymns. They still believed in his reality, which made it even harder to accept his apparent lack of interest in them. They waited for messages from him that did not arrive. They prepared their hearts for meetings that never happened. They listened to other Christians speak as if God showed up every night for supper, leaving them to wonder what they had done wrong to make God go off and start another family.

What most clergy naturally try to do in the face of such pain, she wrote, is to be a substitute for God; blessing, feeding, and forgiving and counseling in his name. Eventually, she decided this was a role that simply did not fit her; to be more real, more human, the clergy collar had to go. With both Taylor and Bailey, their roles as pastor had made them either inhuman or superhuman. To be human, they felt they had to resign.

Unhappy Congregants

The lives of quiet desperation led by these and other pastors are small dots against a giant sheet of seething resentment felt by many churchgoers about their leaders. In an essay, "Sorrow but No Regrets," first published in late July 2007 in *Christianity Today*, Christine Scheller described a thirty-year period in her life of rotten ministers, starting when her pastor hit on her when she was eighteen. She managed to escape him unscathed, but that experience was light compared to another pastor who split the church, then had an affair with a church member. She recounts a succession of pastors who divorced, abused power, engaged in sexual sin, and otherwise betrayed the trust of their flock. She got twenty-four emailed responses to the piece, almost all of them from people who had experienced the same sort of thing she had.

"Are you and I the same person or did we just go to all the same churches?" one wrote.

John Fountain, a former *Washington Post* reporter turned licensed minister and journalism professor at the University of Illinois, blames money-hungry pastors for his disenchantment with the church and subsequent refusal to go. "Mercedes-buying preachers" and husband-and-wife pastoral couples who live off the offerings of poor families, including many single mothers, especially earned his wrath.

Seventy-five percent of the black church is female, he said, a statistic that will only rise as "the church does not—will not—seek us black men out or perhaps even mourn our disappearance from the pews." He complains that the typical black church is irrelevant to the many poor people it serves, and its weekly gatherings are "little more than fundraisers and quasi-fashion shows with a dose of spirituality."

After listing in an essay the numbing amount of work that needs to be done among America's blacks, he wrote:

> I suspect, however that as long as our wives, our children and our money flow through the church's doors, as long as there are still a few bodies to fill the seats, as long as the church can claim a semblance of relevance to the community, as long as some of us on the outside loom as potential critics of the direction, heart and stewardship of those black men charged with leading the church, very few are likely to ever come looking for us.

Inbred Leaders

Sometimes the frustration is aimed at a leadership coterie rather than a single person. When Lifeway Christian Resources polled 469 "formerly churched adults" in 2006 about why they had left, they found the most common reason for not attending church was busy schedules. Second was disenchantment with the pastor or the church. Seventeen percent said church members seemed "hypocritical," another 17 percent said members were "judgmental of others," and 12 percent said the church was run by a clique that discouraged involvement. These adults felt like outsiders looking in.

"Church is set up so you are an audience, and a core group of people do everything," David Frederickson, author of *When the Church Leaves the Building*, said in an interview. "Everyone else feels pretty insignificant. Young Christians can be happy because church appears to lead toward a goal. They are content because they are not burned out yet.

"So you come into a church and it seems loving. But it's a veneer. When you get to know the people—they do the same thing in their marriages unbelievers do, they have the same troubles with pornography and divorce. In fact Christians have a lot of faults the unbelievers don't have."

Now in Sacramento operating a counseling ministry, he added, "The majority of pastors—and I've worked with pastors for years—really are disillusioned and don't believe in a lot of what they are doing. And they do not see any other way. The real question is why the church is in the spiritual state she's in. Why would people want to stay?"

What's happening is a spiritual brain drain, says Alan Jamieson, a researcher who spent four years compiling interviews with 108 "church leavers" in New Zealand for his doctoral thesis on why Christians are fleeing their churches. It's not just the riffraff who are pulling out, he reports in his 2002 book, *A Churchless Faith*; it's many of the strongest Christians in any given church who are heading for the exits. Not only is there no understanding of who leaves and why, but most church leaders don't want to know.

These leaders and pastors are acting more like the hired hand than the good shepherd, he added. "They are happier sitting with the flock than doing the hard work, maybe even personally risky work, of scouring the heights and ledges for those who have wandered off," he wrote. Whereas many businesses court departing customers by asking why they are leaving, church leaders deliberately refuse to ask.

More important to them are the people coming in the front door.

But this is incredibly shortsighted, he adds, as the average leave-takers are in the prime of their lives, at the height of their earning power, skilled workers, and mature in the faith. "As they leave, all the resources they have to give to the life of the church and mission go with them," he wrote. While church leaders bemoan the lack of labor for their outreach ministries, the very people appointed by God to fill such slots "have now slipped out the back door. Imagine the depths of commitment, maturity and trust in God these people would bring to our churches. Losing people like this is nothing short of a tragedy for the church."

Thus what he terms the EPC, for "evangelical-pentecostal-charismatic," churches in the English-speaking world are barely maintaining their numbers. "Working hard to bring new people into the church while letting longer-term highly committed people slip out the back door achieves little," he wrote. "It is time EPC church leaderships woke up."

Linda Eskeldson, a woman living in a small town in southwestern Minnesota, was one such talented leader who got away. Involved with the charismatic movement in the 1970s, she and her family attended various Assemblies of God churches in the 1980s and 1990s. Like a lot of Christians who've been around for a while, she and her husband were not happy with a pastor they considered controlling.

"It was a system that gave the impression it had all the answers and there was no room for questioning," she said. "It was always, 'You don't question the leadership.'"

Such an approach may have worked decades ago, but Christians who remember the excesses of the discipleship movement—utter control of every aspect of people's lives by their leaders—in the mid-1970s have been leery of authoritarian pastors ever since. When Eskeldson's pastor suggested that leave-takers were "stopping the move of God," she fled.

Currently unchurched, her family is looking at a non-traditional church in a college town that is discussion oriented and hierarchically flat.

"I'm not sure the way church is set up now is the way it should be," she said. "Should it be a paid pastor or groups of people who eat together and pray together?"

One of the wisest men I've ever met—who has thought through what being a pastor should be—is Eugene Peterson, a Presbyterian pastor. When I interviewed him in the early 1990s in Pittsburgh, shortly after he penned *The Message*, a well-known New Testament paraphrase, I was impressed by his approachability and his offer to treat me, a poor grad student at the time, to lunch. Years later I read an extraordinary interview he had with *Cutting Edge*, Vineyard Fellowship's magazine for church planters, that covered a wide range of issues. One of his key decisions, he explained, was to reach out to the not-so-influential members instead of catering to the influential and rich.

"Our culture says you go after the winners," he said. "You get the glamorous people. You find the people who are going to help you develop a church. So spend your time with the leaders. . . . But what did Jesus do? He hung out with the losers."

During his twenty-nine years with a Baltimore congregation that went through three building campaigns, one of his elders urged him to pay special attention to the big givers.

"I went away from that and thought, 'You know, I don't think I am going to do that,'" Peterson remembered. "So for the next six months I didn't visit anybody who had any leadership ability or ability to give. I spent my time with the widows, the unemployed, just to break the seduction of that." As it turned out, the money came in anyway.

It's the job of pastors, he added, to know about their sheep and not dump the job on a subordinate. "People deserve to have their name known," he said. "They deserve to have somebody who is a spiritual guide and a preacher and a pastor to them and who has had a cup of coffee in the kitchen. There is so much alienation, so much loneliness around us. Classically, that is what a pastor does. We've lost that. Of course some people think I'm out to lunch because we don't do that in America. We do something big and influential and cost-efficient. Well, a pastoral life is not cost-efficient, I'll tell you. You don't spend three hours in a nursing home and come away feeling like you've been cost-efficient."

One-Man Rule

Jimmy Swaggart's televised confession of sin, delivered on Sunday morning, February 21, 1988, was one of the most dramatic pieces of religious theater I have ever seen. I had jumped on a plane for Baton Rouge the afternoon before so I could show up at the rose-carpeted Family Worship Center the next morning to cover it for the *Houston Chronicle*. I was mesmerized and horrified by this man sobbing before the TV cameras and seventy-five hundred of us in the sanctuary, his wife sitting there dressed in bright pink. Clearly the church members, who gave him ten ovations, resented the presence of reporters.

"So many would ask, Why? Why?" Swaggart said between sobs. "I've asked that myself ten thousand times through ten thousand tears. Maybe it was because Jimmy Swaggart tried to live his entire life as if he was not human . . . as if there was nothing I could not do. And I think this is the reason . . . I did not find the victory that I sought because I did not seek the help of my brothers and sisters in the Lord."

He added, "This gospel is flawless even though it is min-istered at times by flawed men."

Eighteen years later, when news about the sexual misdeeds of Ted Haggard, pastor of New Life Church in Colorado Springs, hit the news, it was déjà vu: the horrific rumors from a local television station, the vague statements from the church, the reporters who showed up to try to wring more details out of a contrite evangelist. Unlike Swaggart, Haggard forewent a colorful final act and instead sent a farewell letter, which was read to his tearful congregation on November 5, 2006.

"The public person I was wasn't a lie," Haggard wrote, "it was just incomplete. When I stopped communicating about my problems, the darkness increased and finally dominated me. As a result, I did things that were contrary to everything I believe."

Both Swaggart and Haggard said they were caught up in a pretend world, unable to confide about the real issues in their lives. In 2005 Haggard told *Charisma* magazine that pastors are the reason the laity leave the church. "They have been let down by church leaders whose children are wild and disobedient or who are in adulterous marriages," *Charisma* quoted him as saying.

How could Haggard have been so out of touch? In July 2006 pollster George Barna produced the results of a poll of 627 senior pastors of Protestant churches taken in the fall of 2005. One thing that jumped out was that 61 percent of those polled admitted they have "few close friends."

One out of five was dealing with "very difficult" family problems, one-quarter described themselves as introverts, and one-sixth felt underappreciated.

These pastors were also questioned about the spiritual health of their congregations, as were a group of 1002 adult laypeople. Two very different perspectives emerged. Pastors guessed that 70 percent of their members placed their faith in God as their top priority. The members' survey showed it was more like 23 percent.

When asked to measure the spiritual vitality of their congregations, pastors listed such things as reactions to their sermons, a born-again experience, church and Sunday school attendance. They had missed the boat, according to Barna, as the pastors should have been asking more discerning questions, such as whether their members tithed, evangelized, and led godly lifestyles.

"There is a huge gap between the perception of pastors and the reality of people's devotion to God," the pollster said in a statement released with the poll. "Pastors evaluate spiritual health from an institutional perspective—that is, are people involved in keeping the system going—while people are aware of their unmet need to have a deeper and more meaningful relationship with God."

Barna says most pastors are not leaders. They may be teachers or shepherds, but they do not lead—that is, motivate the flock and lead institutional change. They are not entrepreneurs; if anything, their business model would be to do nothing at all or the least amount of change possible. They are by nature risk-averse personalities. This would be deadly in the business world, and it's deadly in the kingdom of God as well.

Fifteen years before, Rick Joyner, a pastor and teacher in Charlotte, North Carolina, came to the same conclusion. In a series on leadership in his *Morning Star* publication, he explained that churches must be led, not managed.

"Just having vision is not enough," he wrote. "Many who have vision and can understand the consequences of their actions do not have the will or spiritual fortitude to implement those actions." Moreover, he added, "To properly understand leadership, we must first distinguish it from management.

Confusing management with leadership has caused many a church, ministry or enterprise to seize defeat from the jaws of victory."

Joyner calls on the pastor to keep the big picture before the congregation, as well as be a person whose true spiritual authority means influence with God. The perfect solution for a church, he added, is what he calls a union of prophetic and teaching ministries in the church, where the managers and the visionaries balance out each other.

Revolt of the Laity

Pam and Dick Ewing, the couple I interviewed in Winthrop, Washington, say there's a natural way to deal with the inevitable failures that a pastor will have. Dick's initial vision was for a large team of elders to lead a church and take turns preaching. Decisions would not be announced until the elders could agree on them. Each elder could focus on his strengths and let others step in where he was weak. No one person was allowed to be in control. Building on an eldership system is much more time-consuming than the one-man church, but it would do one thing most churches do not do well: provide enough leaders to pastor and disciple the people. Dick said that one-on-one interaction with an elder is how lives are changed.

To his surprise, the local congregations, like the Israelites in Samuel's day, did not want to be ruled by a panel of judges. Instead, they wanted a take-charge pastor. Dick eventually threw in the towel. "If I'm going to be a bench warmer and be there mainly to cheer on the pastor and pay his salary but have no say in what goes on, why should I go?" he asked. Men especially, he added, don't like being passive, so they quickly dismiss a controlling pastor.

One facet of control is secrecy. I've learned from years of religion reporting that many churches are very reluctant to give out their annual budget figures. Even worse, pastors do not want to divulge their salaries, even to the congregants who are paying the bills. Pastors are traditionally as poor as church mice, but usually for those who oversee a large church, salaries are generous. I learned this from reading "Innovation 2007," a glossy booklet produced by the Dallas-based Leadership Network. In 2006 the network, in collaboration with *Church Executive* magazine, surveyed 56 churches with an attendance of 1,500 or more. The average senior pastor's salary was $132,000, the executive pastor averaged $90,000, associate pastors averaged $82,000, business administrators averaged $74,000, and worship leaders got $73,000. This is significantly above the earnings of a typical American. It's a valid question to ask if pastors are at all in touch with the realities their congregations face when they can afford private schools and significantly better housing.

As for the small-church, poorly paid pastor, well-known evangelist David Wilkerson has a heart for them. Many pastors' conferences emphasize megachurch growth, he writes, which only causes the smaller church pastors to become more and more discouraged, feeling nothing they do is really significant.

But often the megachurch pastor ignores the hurting and needy people whom Christ loves, Wilkerson wrote in an April 2005 newsletter. Moreover, the chasm between the large-church and small-church pastor is un-Christlike. He quotes Zechariah 4:10: "Who hath despised the day of small things?"

When I interviewed him in 1998, he told me he gets letters from anguished people—fifty to seventy-five thousand letters a month—who have no pastor and nowhere to turn. He also counseled many pastors. Most of their problems, he reported, are sexual. Porn was "the number one problem in ministry," he said.

"It's the discouragement," he added. "The pastors are having a hard time because their people are having such exotic problems. . . . Tragically, Christians seem to be as troubled as are the masses of the unconverted. We're losing ground that was already won."

"Many ministers are alone, discouraged and ready to quit," wrote his son, Gary, in a 2006 addendum to one of his father's newsletters. "In one of our meetings, over two hundred pastors came for prayer, confessing they were preparing to quit the ministry immediately. So many today feel like failures because they think they're not doing enough. The church leaders of our generation need an extraordinary infusion of encouragement."

My research boils down to two intractable problems. One is unhappy pastors who feel they cannot begin to fill the job description set out for them, who have a church government setup that does not work, and who every day encounter problems that would test Solomon himself. The other is laity who wonder if their spiritual leaders have real lives. They have had it with pastors who have no clue what a typical workday is like or what it's like to commute, put up with day care, or deal with numerous other challenges that most of the congregation must face every day. Few pastors have worked on the corporate level, and therefore they don't understand the challenges of having standing in the work world. Instead, their ministers keep office hours during time slots when it's impossible for working people to get there. They have a lot of flexible, unsupervised time, unlike most of their parishioners.

What many believe to be the best solution going at present—the house-church movement—is essentially a revolt against pastors and even parachurch groups.

Gwen, a retired missionary and single mom from Salem, Oregon, said her pastor ignored her because she was an obviously needy single mother.

"The churches I've been involved with were not very aware of singles and the elderly," she said. "They were constantly hitting up the middle class, the married who were their bread and butter. I never felt connected. I tried hard: helped in the food bank, volunteered for the missions committee, went to Sunday school. I didn't want to go to a church feeling like I've wasted my time. The sermons were the same old, same old.

"People used to say I needed to get more involved. I said, what more do I need to do? I am involved in lots of things. When I ended up in the hospital with my cancer surgery, no one came to visit me. Does this just happen in the right-wing denominations? I have a friend who goes to the Episcopal Church, and they always let her know there that they miss her."

About her house church she said, "I am so excited and on fire when we meet. Our Bible study is in-depth, we all get to ask questions, we all care about each other, and we all find the one-on-one the church was meant to be."

Judging from hers and other anecdotes, such meetings will remain spiritually fulfilling as long as they remain decentralized, spiritually available, and not too attached to a denomination. "Many denominations are movements that have stopped moving," Joyner noted in his article. "As soon as a movement starts taking an identity other than Christ, it has opened the door to the control spirit. The control spirit then begins exerting pressure to conform to the image of the movement instead of seeking to conform the followers to the image of Christ." And this is where the rub occurs. Congregations that have lost their vision stagnate to the point where many of the true believers depart. They cannot stand that spirit of control, and they aren't picking up the fragrance of Christ anywhere near the place.

So where does that leave us? Haddon Robinson, the seminary president, said, "The pastor of a growing Protestant church has one of the most difficult jobs in Christendom because it demands so much variety in order to do it well. Three years in seminary can't begin to prepare a person for this multifaceted job."

This is why my sympathies are with people who propose an eldership form of church governance. Too many people are crashing and burning under the current pastor-does-all system. Of course the pastor has to agree to share power; something not all clergy are willing to do. If the minister insists on doing it all, he or she must accept the inevitable burnout that comes with maintaining tight control.

Haddon made a key point: "A lot of pastors are all circumference and no center. If you are going to preach well, you have to spend time studying."

Time alone, time spent with God, time spent in the Bible—pastors who fight for this time manage not only to produce better sermons but also to keep their personality centered on God. When they slip off that center, that's when the worst problems arise.

8

THE OTHER SEX

Why Many Women Are Fed Up

In the 1990s the big trend—and worry—in the church was that men were heading out the back door. There was David Murrow's book *Why Men Hate Going to Church*. There was Leon Podles's *The Church Impotent*, about the feminization of the church. Then there was Scott Pinzon's hilarious piece in the August 1999 issue of *CBA Marketplace*. He called Christian bookstores "death by estrogen." He wrote:

> The typical evangelical bookshop is a disaster for men, stocked with pink and lavender "Precious Moments" figures, acres of children's books, cash registers decorated in mauve and rose, sentimental paintings on the walls and arrays of "home decor froufrou." Wouldn't it have been cheaper and easier just to spray the whole store with a jumbo, extra-strength can of man repellent?

Murrow's and Podles's books did well, and judging by the situation today, many church leaders got the hint. There was a swing away from the feminine, judging by the way some houses of worship are set up like sports bars with Toshiba screens and refreshments, and others serve up content in abbreviated portions, all for the supposedly shorter attention spans of men.

The more I looked at churches, though, I found women were leaving as well. This came as a surprise, as Murrow portrayed the typical church as catering to women's needs, not a huge surprise in that more than 60 percent of the adults at a typical worship service are women, which translates into thirteen million more women than men in the pews on any given Sunday.

Then a young woman I will call Rachael dropped by my office. She was a graduate of a well-known Pentecostal university and had a few years of working in the Washington media under her belt. Dissatisfied with what churches offered people like her, she went to Europe for a master's degree and an escape from her evangelical ghetto. There the anti-Americanism blindsided her at first, but she adjusted.

When she returned two years later, nearly all her Christian girlfriends had married and were working on their first pregnancy. Their attitude was that, while the good men get snapped up early, one can always pick up a career. None of these friends shared her vision for transforming society or building up a Christian influence in the culture, goals that often demand a lot of energy during that same key time period in one's twenties.

What really got to Rachael was how her friends' choices were lauded by the Christian community, while hers were not.

"The Christian world puts everyone in a little box and has no time for people who step outside it," she groused over lunch in my company cafeteria. "They believe you need to get married young and have lots of kids. They have no paradigm for anyone who steps outside that box."

No Significant Place

If you are a woman, do all churches shove you off to the side, unless you're married with babies? Or even if you do fall within that revered category, are you stuck for life with teaching Sunday school? I began talking with women, married and single, of various ethnicities, about what they were getting or not getting from their churches.

I sought out Sarah Zacharias Davis, daughter of evangelist Ravi Zacharias and the author of two recent books, *Confessions of an Honest Wife* and *Transparent: Getting Honest about Who We Are*, that include many interviews with women.

"Women don't feel there is any kind of significant place in the church where they are really valued," she told me. "At the end of the day, all they want them to do is teach Sunday school. All the bigger positions are given to men. Women want to do more."

As for the independent and career-driven women she interviewed, "There is not a place for them in the church," she reported. "The only thing modeled in the church is the traditional model of the man being in charge of the home. There is not really a shared partnership. There's even more of that in the South, where I live. But I've interviewed women across the country and everywhere it's the same story. And it is the younger women who are complaining about it."

Few of these women officially leave church, she said. They just don't attend. Shut off from the kinds of ministry that interested her, she left her old church because she felt she never was giving anything to it that really mattered. She now attends St. Philip's Episcopal Cathedral in Atlanta. "I respect the fact that they ordain women," she said—not that she wants to be ordained. "They consider women equal in value."

I asked if she could name one evangelical woman who she knew was satisfied with her church. She could not.

Sometimes being recognized as a leader doesn't solve things either. I met with Robbi Kenney, a friend from seminary days who was a pioneer in the ex-gay movement and a cofounder of Exodus International. As a straight woman, she was involved with a segment of people most churches would not touch. Her efforts to get ordained ran aground, she told me, when she was wrongly accused of adultery by an anonymous person in the Episcopal Diocese of Pittsburgh. She was dismissed from the ordination process, while the men with whom she was alleged to be involved were ordained and placed in parishes.

Now making movies in Los Angeles, she says she can almost laugh about that part of her life, but it's been years since she's darkened the door of a church. Being female and a leader was a major problem.

"I always needed a place where I was accepted and could be useful," she says. "I don't think it's healthy being in a place where you're constantly rejected. . . . It was clear to me early on I could never follow a narrow concept of what a woman is."

Women like Kenney—and there are more and more of them these days—do not fit in either liberal or conservative churches. The more conservative ones don't allow them into any leadership posts that have anything to do with teaching, but the theology in the liberal ones is untenable to them.

"I've always had a problem with the conservative culture that leads toward Republicanism, since I am a social liberal," Kenney says. "I prefer churches that believe women can be in leadership, and that's a fading star in conservative circles. My theology remains orthodox, but I don't fit in conservative circles and am not comfortable in liberal ones."

Masks of Perfection

According to George Barna's March 2006 survey on un-churched America, men represent the majority of un-churched adults at 55 percent, but over the past decade there was a "significant" increase in women who avoid church. "Since 1991, the percentage of unchurched women has gone from 18 to 30 percent," stated Pennsylvania author Dannah Gresh in her 2005 book.

> Today's overextended woman has no patience for a powerless, impersonal church experience. Among those who are sticking it out, half are still desperately trying to find a few close friends. Twenty-five percent of those say they feel discouraged and depressed. They're stuck behind masks of perfection.

I thought of Sarah Zacharias Davis's books, which have such a current of sadness running through them. "That's because women said how they felt," she told me, "not what they were supposed to feel."

Well, where do women fit in church? The Pentecostals do better than average at inclusion. One of the first ministers to pioneer female leaders was David Yonggi Cho, pastor of the 763,000-strong Yoido Full Gospel Church in Seoul.

Four hundred of his 600 associate pastors are women, as are 47,000 of his 50,000 cell group leaders.

Then there are women like Carolyn Custis James, a member of the Presbyterian Church of America (one of the most conservative denominations around when it comes to women's roles), president of the Whitby Forum, and author of the 2002 book *When Life and Beliefs Collide*. It was the first book I read that encouraged women to get a theological education. Her husband, Frank James, is president of the Reformed Theological Seminary in Orlando.

How does she swim upstream, I wondered, especially after a ruckus following her February 2006 speech at Covenant College, a PCA school? In the speech she had suggested women are not limited solely to ministering to other women in church and their callings are not limited to being wives and mothers. Then she named conference speaker Joni Eareckson Tada and authors Nancy Pearcey and Susan Hunt as examples of female theologians who are making a major impact on the PCA as well as the broader evangelical world.

"The stewardship of women's gifts is a huge issue we cannot avoid," she said. "It is a serious matter to Jesus when talents are buried in the ground. But an equally important issue is the simple fact that both men and women need the spiritual ministries women offer."

In response to a question following her presentation, Carolyn James agreed with a young female student that the discussion over gender roles in the church is often stifled or guarded due to fear in both men and women.

"Men are afraid they will lose their male authority," James said, "or women are afraid they will be seen as 'bad.' What I see as the 'blessed alliance' between men and women doesn't diminish men at all."

She was soon called on the cyber carpet by David Bayly, a Toledo, Ohio, PCA pastor who wrote "Come Out from Behind Those Skirts: An Open Letter to Frank James" on his BaylyBlog asking if Mrs. James's husband was fully aware of his wife's theological errors and whether she was submitted to him.

A month later, Randy Stinson, executive director of the Council on Biblical Manhood and Womanhood, posted a critique. "We are certainly glad that someone is addressing the issue of empowering women to use their God-given gifts in the church and fully support that biblical idea," he wrote in an essay posted March 27, 2006, on www.gender-news.com. "However, there is a clear complementary framework within the fabric of Scripture that must serve as the foundation for the way in which both men and women use those gifts in the church. God's Word has given us much clear guidance on this and we must not move beyond it."

I called up James to get her side of the story. She told me many women have long since taken their talents outside the church.

"I'm in a denomination that isn't about to ordain women, so I don't talk about that question," she said. "In denominations that do ordain females, women are still having problems, so there's a deeper issue here. Even in more liberal churches where women still have a place at the table, their presence doesn't mean as much as that of a man."

After her 2002 book, she began meeting women who had taken her advice to get that master's degree even though there was nowhere they could use it at their churches. Intrigued, she conducted an informal poll of PCA women.

"Generally, I am hearing women don't feel there is a place for them at the church," she said. "Women CEOs are told to take a turn in the nursery. I talked with a lawyer for whom the only job they had for her at the church was the receptionist. I know one woman who approached church elders to form a support group for women in crisis, but they turned her down. They said, 'Women will gossip.' Women are sent to either help at Sunday school, with mercy ministries or the women's ministry. That's like telling men they can just be handymen, ushers, or help with the Boys Club.

"So, seminary educated women are taking their ministries elsewhere. Like me, I am on the road and writing books. There is not much I am doing in terms of the local church. Other women are just creating 501-c3s and doing ministry from there. Others are heading back into the secular world. There is a disconnect between being a young woman on a college campus, and when you graduate and try to be involved in church, only to find out you are not wanted."

Such women, she added, need to be mobilized and given a vision for God's call on their lives, not pushed away. Some male leaders are so fixated on opposing women's ordination, "they can't talk about other things," she said. "Every time they give ground to women, it's seen as caving in to the other side.

"There are some amazing men out there who get it, but generally speaking, women are not taken seriously," she concluded. "They don't want to usurp, they want to be part of a team. We do want men to be strong, to step up. But you need strong women too."

Women are blossoming in the blogosphere, where there's no one to quash them. Catholics Amy Welborn and Dawn Eden are two examples. One blog, called "emerging women," listed items like "Fifty ways to encourage a woman leader." A variety of under-forty women were exchanging ideas in this forum, some of whom fit the "type" James was talking about. One said she had been to seminary, was ordained, had written her master's thesis on female Pentecostals, but "am not currently pastoring a church or am in any active ministry." She too was on the shelf.

"So many evangelical churches do not allow women any significant role," said Brian McLaren, of Cedar Ridge Community Church. "For someone to be in a world where men and women are equal and then to enter a world where they aren't—it feels less moral than the world you were in. It's like entering a club where everyone is racist. You are embarrassed to be there."

When I talked with Michael Lindsay, the Rice University professor who interviewed 360 elite evangelical leaders, I looked at the index and noticed very few female names. His interview ratio, he admitted, was 90 percent men and 10 percent women.

"Women are under-represented in the evangelical elite, period," he said.

One of Our Fifty Is Missing

In September 2006, when *Christianity Today* came out with a cover story on how Reformed theology is sweeping through evangelical churches, a reporter was soon standing by my desk, asking to borrow the issue. I too was interested in this phenomenon. A theology most of us had relegated to the right of Francis Schaeffer was now the thought *du jour* in lots of growing urban churches.

I glanced at the photo by Peter Artemenko that accompanied the article of a gathering of Reformed pastors, and of course one thing stood out immediately. The only people I could see in that room were men. Okay, it was a pastors' conference. But all the leaders of this neo-Calvinist movement listed in the sidebar were men. Other than a female seeker quoted at the beginning of the piece, all the conversation was between men. Were women being relegated to the back of the bus in this new evangelical wave?

I checked some other issues of *Christianity Today*. In its update on Christian publishing in the June 2007 issue, the list of bestselling Christian books were all by male authors with the exception of Denver evangelist Joyce Meyer. Colorado Springs writer Stasi Eldredge was also listed as a co-writer (for her book *Captivating*) with her better-known husband, John. That same issue had Donald Miller, the postmodern author of *Blue Like Jazz*, on the cover. How many female authors have appeared on the cover of *Christianity Today*?

This is not to say Christian women do not write. They do, and there are immensely talented ones who have a lot to say. In addition to the aforementioned women in this chapter, there's also Frederica Mathewes-Green, who writes on Orthodoxy and pro-life issues; the multitalented College of William and Mary professor Susan Wise Bauer; Carmelite nun and art critic Sister Wendy Beckett; Houston author Anita Higman, who writes everything from Christian romance novels to Texas history; and Miriam Adeney, a Seattle college professor who has carved out a niche on how to minister to Muslim women. These are women who have gotten published through their own merits, not because they are wives of famous husbands. But I rarely see their books advertised. I belong to a group of journalists who cover religion. At our yearly conferences, evangelical publishers will sponsor a lunch or break featuring a top author we can interview. Rarely do those publishers present a female author.

I was paging through yet another issue of *Christianity Today* in the latter part of 2006 when I saw an ad for a Robert Schuller conference called "Faith Forward." I glanced at the speakers: there were white faces, black faces. A lot of the men were successful pastors of megachurches or emergent congregations. Some were trend watchers; one was a futurist; one even worked in the National Human Genome Research Institute in Bethesda, Maryland. Out of eighteen people listed, the only woman was Arvella Schuller, wife of the organizer. Was it possible organizers for this conference couldn't find any other female thinker to invite who could speak on the topic of the changing mission of the church?

Then there was the ad in *Charisma*'s December 2006 issue about a "Creative Church Conference" led by Grapevine, Texas, pastor Ed Young for the following February. The speakers were Mark Driscoll of Seattle's Mars Hill; Bishop T. D. Jakes of The Potter's House in Dallas; Ed Young of Houston's Second Baptist Church; and Craig Groeschel, founding and senior pastor of Life Church in Edmond, Oklahoma. I checked the conference website, edyoung.com. Sure enough, there were no women listed. Does this group think women have nothing to say to them?

I picked up the November 2007 copy of *Touchstone*, an Orthodox Christian journal based in Chicago, which featured a symposium of six evangelical thinkers. All were men, as were all the senior editors. I was glad to see they had a female managing editor, but couldn't they do better?

I was reminded of a column in *New Mexico* magazine called "One of Our Fifty Is Missing." It's a wry collection of quotes from people and newspapers about how everyone from plane reservations agents to television newscasters forgets that New Mexico has been a state since 1912. They think it's part of Mexico, so anyone booking a flight to Albuquerque is told it's an international flight. Or the state gets mistaken for Arizona. Every month, the editors run a column listing all the bloopers that occur nationwide.

A similar situation has happened in church. Sometimes it seems like there's a whole gender missing. Back in 1998 I was interviewing David Wilkerson, famed author of *The Cross and the Switchblade*, when I brought up the annual calendar his ministry puts out that has a biblical promise for every day of the year. Why, I asked, were there never any quotes from promises in the Bible that employ female pronouns, such as the speech by Elizabeth in Luke 1:45? Or Matthew 9:22 and Luke 8:48, which also have female pronouns—and a wonderful promise? Or the verse on barrenness in Isaiah 54:1? Wilkerson did not respond. To date, I have yet to see such verses; a quick read of the 2006 and 2007 promise calendars did not reveal them—except for Isaiah 54:4, which refers to widowhood. Sure there are lots of Bible verses with promises, but these are notable omissions. Are women so poisonous that they are not allowed even one biblical reference?

Potential Temptresses

In the Washington metropolitan area on any given day, 45 percent of the customers at local supermarkets don't know what they are having for dinner until 4 p.m. Groceries' busiest weekday hours are 4–8 p.m., and Sundays are the busiest shopping day of the week, in direct competition with church. More and more workplaces operate twenty-four hours a day, seven days a week, and people must adjust their schedules to this. The *Washington Post* reported that a poll of nearly eight hundred working women, released March 9, 2000, by the AFL-CIO, charted how forty-six of the women surveyed work opposite or contrasting shifts to their husband or partner; one out of four work in the evenings or weekends; and many have workplaces that do not provide child-care benefits, paid maternity leave, or flexibility with their hours, much less retirement benefits. In a grinder like this, what's going to drop out of schedule is church, especially if it's seen as a time-waster or an added stressor.

What if these women want to meet with their pastor to seek counsel over a problem? Many pastors follow Billy Graham's model and refuse to meet with a woman alone for any reason whatsoever. This sounds virtuous, but it disenfranchises half the congregation. A professional woman would be wildly insulted if a male business associate suggested she was a potential temptress. Yet women are supposed to put up with this in a church setting.

"Women are considered dangerous, so they are shunned," Carolyn James told me. "Men think, *Well, it's Eve who got us into this mess we're in.*"

"One of the things we've gotten so spooked about is sexual transgression by the pastor," said longtime Presbyterian pastor and author Eugene Peterson in a 2002 interview with *Cutting Edge* magazine. "I think we start at the wrong end. The genius of a pastor is his capacity for intimacy, his willingness to be intimate. But if your imagination is so shaped by the culture, shaped by its ideas of sex, then every woman is either a temptation or a threat. Usually they are neither."

There does seem to be a huge disconnect between what women are reputed to be and what they are. Southwestern Baptist Theological Seminary in Ft. Worth got lots of publicity and raised eyebrows about its new academic program on homemaking that began in the fall 2007 semester. The twenty-three hours of course work, which are part of a BA in humanities, include classes on how to cook, sew, raise children, and oversee a "biblical model for the home and family." The classes are for women only. Seminary President Paige Patterson, a former president of the Southern Baptist

Convention, claimed that wives of seminary students asked for the course, according to the Associated Press.

Seminary officials also told reporters there are nine other women's programs at the seminary, and this one is specifically for women called to minister in the home. After all, the SBC had passed a resolution in 2000 saying wives should "graciously submit" to their husbands. Then in March 2007, Sheri Klouda, one of their former theology professors, sued the school in federal court for firing her from her tenured position as a Hebrew instructor simply because of her gender.

Visit a bookstore in a conservative church and note the number of books written by women. Two large Reformed congregations I visited have about one hundred titles by men and three by women. The latter are either on child rearing or written in tandem with their husbands. The message to women is: their role is that of wife and mother. But according to 2004 census data, 44.6 percent of all women between the ages of fifteen and forty-four are childless, up from 35 percent in 1976. Is there no place in church for these women? Isn't that a huge number of people to write off?

As for women needing to be wives, churches are notorious for not having enough Christian men to go around. So what are the remaining women supposed to do?

"If you walk into the church on the arm of a man, you have a different place than if you walk in by yourself," James told me, and single women can spot the double standard in a heartbeat. Although they are scorned by the church, one group still wants single women: politicians. Only nineteen million single women voted in 2000, but their numbers skyrocketed to twenty-seven million in the 2004 election. In 2008 this demographic will number at least thirty-three million women if they all vote. In the New Hampshire primary in January 2008, single women voted in "historic" numbers, mostly for Hillary Clinton, according to Women's Voices, Women Vote, a voter registration group for single women. If politicians are tapping into women's know-how and clout, why can't the church? More truthfully, why *won't* the church?

On a personal level, I have been one of those unwanted women for years. At my last church, the only avenues open to me were child care, altar guild, or the greeters ministry, even though I traveled for work and could not commit to being at the church every week. I did offer to do things that fit my schedule, such as help with the liturgical dance ministry, play the harp before the worship service, or share insights from my 1998 children's book with young moms. All my overtures were ignored or turned down.

No one had a vision for my journalistic calling, even though my articles reached more people on a given day than most pastors hope to reach in a year. Instead, people told me to my face they couldn't stand the newspaper I worked for. While I was the only layperson in the church who had a seminary degree, I was never asked to teach or lead anything, not even the singles ministry. After two years of attending the church, I stopped offering my services. Instead, I posted my newest singles essays on Prison Fellowship's *Breakpoint* website. I joined the international board of a ministry to Christian journalists and became its vice president. I also invested seven years assisting Kurdish immigrants, who were grateful for anything I could give. After five years of attending the church, I left.

I would not feel as though I really belonged in a church until years later, when I adopted a little girl. Finally I was in a role other Christians could accept.

9

◇◇◇◇◇◇◇◇

BEWILDERED CHARISMATICS

Looking for the Spirit in a Parched Land

It was a snowy February morning in a small town about two hundred miles south of the Russian border. I was in the far north of Kazakhstan, the largest of the former Soviet Union's republics, and on the southwestern corner of the vast Siberian plain that covers much of Asia. I had been in the country about four weeks at this point, adopting a child with hazel eyes and tousled brown hair. I had nicknamed her Veeka. This was our first vacation trip together.

It was the beginning of 2007, and I had been living in Kostenai, the largest city in the region. I bumped into Masha, an eighteen-year-old college student who invited my daughter and me to come to the much smaller town of Lisakovsk for the weekend. She had translated for me when I was stuck at a department store, trying to buy new toddler clothes using my very poor Russian. When I took her out to lunch, she volunteered that she and her family attended a charismatic church.

"Charismatic?" I said. I knew Pentecostals were world-wide, but never did I think I'd hear anyone use the word *charismatic* in this obscure corner of central Asia. Not only did Masha attend the church, she was on the worship team.

About a week later, there I was at Lisakovsk Christian Family Center, a lively fellowship founded by an entrepreneurial Canadian. Donald Wallis had moved to Kazakhstan years ago to sell thrashers, a wheat harvesting instrument for the kind of cold climates he weathered while growing up in Saskatchewan. Not content with the local Orthodox churches there, he had founded his own congregation and had trained the local Kazakhs how to run a Sunday school and sing praise music. Wallis preached the sermon that day, and I remember him saying he still encountered people who opposed the more controversial gifts of the Holy Spirit, such as speaking in tongues, but that he would plow ahead with his church anyway.

I sat there, in the middle of nowhere, seven thousand miles and eleven time zones away from home, immersed in the Russian praise music. Here was a church that was growing and where people welcomed the Holy Spirit, a switch from much of the church scene in the United States.

As I've talked with people about why they have left church, I've found one unspoken undercurrent in several conversations. It lies somewhere between disappointment and detachment, a remembrance of things past that are no more. These are the people who say they joined at a time when they would merely walk into a church and their lives would be drastically changed by the Holy Spirit. The scene is so different now that for some, it hurts too much to go back.

There was a time in the memory of almost everyone over forty when churches were filled, Christian coffeehouses were booming, and one could scarcely take a step in the downtown of any major American city without someone coming up to witness or preach. This was the time of the Jesus Movement, which kicked off in the late 1960s, when all sorts of hippies started getting saved. Their conversions changed the face of American Christianity. Music and worship styles were dramatically transformed. Denominations were birthed. The media reported on mass baptisms in the California surf and the rise of evangelical social-action groups. Sports stadiums were filled, climaxing with the enormous July 1977 Conference on the Charismatic Renewal in the Christian Churches, when forty-five thousand worshipers rocked Kansas City.

My friend "Maeve" and I were eating lunch one day when she reminded me about the glory days of the charismatic movement that so transformed the church back then.

"A lot of us remember what it was like when the Holy Spirit was flowing down. Now we can't bear to see the ashes," she was telling me over a tomato and tuna salad. She and her husband had finally settled at a church that doesn't even try to replicate the wonders but presents a gorgeous music program to make up for the lack of spiritual power.

What confounded Maeve, she said, "are the outright promises in the Bible that lead us to expect answered prayer. These are things that are right there in the Word." She wonders if somehow she misinterpreted what Jesus said.

I pointed out that all four of the Gospel writers included Jesus's sweeping promises in the ask-whatever-you-will-in-my-name-and-I-will-do-it category.

"If he didn't mean it, why did he say it?" I asked.

This same topic came up in my interviews with Brian McLaren. "Unanswered prayer is a huge issue," he said. "A certain kind of charismatic and Pentecostal theology has promised miracles on demand and it's not worked." Listing a series of famous charismatic leaders who had encountered public disgrace, mostly over sexual sins, he noted, "What they're all saying is that when push came to shove, it didn't work for them." When the going got rough on the sexual front, the spiritual power was not there to overcome the temptation.

Raising the Flag

I've mentioned before a large 2001 worship conference in Kansas City I attended some time back. During the final day, I met with Mike Bickle, founder of the International House of Prayer—along with about nine other members of his team—in his hotel suite for an interview.

I asked him how they had so effortlessly blended worship and the use of the spiritual gifts. I noticed how worship leaders came up with sung prophecies at the drop of a hat; people could make appointments with prayer teams to receive a "word of knowledge" about one's personal life (I saw people walking into these sessions with tape recorders); and a Middle Eastern worship CD I had picked up in the conference bookstore had a long aria in tongues. These people seemed to move naturally in this realm in contrast to everywhere else I'd been, where such spiritual phenomena were no longer welcome.

"In theory," he said, "people repeat what they've seen at this conference when they go back home to their churches, but in reality, this is an oasis in the desert."

One team member chimed in to mention that several visitors to the conference were from a new denomination that had started out as charismatic in the 1970s but that "now," she said, "their pastors are all into control."

I had to admit that Bickle had not hogged the microphone at this conference, only occasionally coming forward for instruction or to give directions.

"There are enough people watching what we're doing here," he said, "and there are a million or two out there who see us raising the flag."

That conference had drawn a category of people whom I'd call bewildered charismatics. Some church historians have compared the Jesus Movement to a third Great Awakening (the first two having occurred circa 1730 and 1801), when Pentecostal power exploded into the mainline churches. Although people were no less sinless back then than they are now, miracles of all sorts happened.

But the music died, and no one I've talked with seems to know why. The consensus is that the Holy Spirit gets quenched more often than not on Sunday mornings, supposedly because the manifestations might scare off any newcomers. Actually newcomers are quite intrigued. While researching a book on one very overtly charismatic church, I kept running into people who had walked in as rank atheists and were thunderstruck by some prophecy or message in tongues/interpretation that applied specifically to them.

The power engine behind all that revival began at the turn of the century with the founding of the Pentecostal movement on New Year's Day, 1901. That is when a group of Bible students in a small mission in west Topeka, Kansas, were searching to be baptized in the Holy Spirit. Searching the New Testament, they deduced that when the apostles had prayed thus for people, more often than not, they spoke in tongues. They began praying over each other for this blessing and first one woman, Agnes Ozman, then others in the group began praying in tongues. No longer was this gift for a select few; it was for everyone, and from that moment on, it became linked with the baptism of the Holy Spirit. Thus was the Pentecostal movement born in the early hours of the twentieth century.

Most Christians violently disagreed with this movement, and for decades Pentecostals hung about the fringes of the Christian community. About sixty years later, in April 1960, Pentecostalism hit the mainline denominations when an Episcopal priest, Dennis Bennett, announced to his Van Nuys, California, church that he had been given the gift of speaking in tongues after having experienced this spiritual baptism. He was forced to resign from his church, his story ended up on television and in *Time* and *Newsweek*, and he ended up at St. Luke's Episcopal in Seattle, which became a world-famous renewal center.

Bennett and other clergy who were testing out this new movement spent the 1960s telling people from all denominations of this fabulous experience that felt like Acts 2 coming to life. People were finding references, in code as it were, to the baptism in the Spirit throughout the New Testament, and once-mysterious passages in the letters to the Corinthians and the Galatians made sense when seen through a charismatic lense. Those letters, it seemed, were aimed at people who had had this experience. By the time Paul penned these missives from prison, "receiving the Holy Spirit," as it was termed at the time, was assumed to be part of the Christian experience. This is the reason the theology of it all was not explained step-by-step for the benefit of readers nineteen centuries in the future who had not lived through Acts 2.

But by the late 1960s, many hippies were ready to hear about Christ, and the ground had been laid in terms of the Pentecostal gifts being available if one knew what church or prayer meeting to go to. And again the era seemed like Acts 2 come to life, especially in the founding of many charismatic

Christian communities where people shared their wealth and possessions, as did the early Christians. More often than not, these experiments did not last long, but they were valiant attempts at getting back to the basics.

The Flames Dim

Years later, I delved into the history of this movement as part of my master's thesis and found that 1977 was the apex of this renewal, at least within U.S. borders. The Kansas City conference was an impressive gathering of every denomination under the sun—a feat no organization had pulled off until then. It had outdone the National Council of Churches in bringing together Catholics, Protestants, Orthodox, and Messianic Jews in a way nothing else had. According to many, it was the most promising thing to happen in American religion since the Second Great Awakening in 1801.

The thinking at the time was that the movement would move from strength to strength. Instead, I learned, there were splits between leaders, especially within the Catholic charismatic renewal. The mainline Protestant charismatics were chagrined to see a new breed of nondenominational churches spring up and lure away their most committed members. Then in the late 1980s, charismatics suffered a near deathblow when some of their most famous televangelists went up in flames, after being outed for sexual misdeeds. The renewal never recovered from that.

By the early 1990s baby boomer Christians were desperate for a repeat of all the spiritual phenomena they had grown up with. Then in 1994 a phenomenon known as the "Toronto blessing" hit the news. The host church, the Toronto Airport Vineyard, became famous because of "holy laughter," apparently uncontrollable peals of mirth people had during meetings. This and even stranger phenomena that originated at this church were totally new in the charismatic world.

Added to that was the entrance of South African evangelist Rodney Howard Browne, also an originator of the holy laughter movement. I did an investigation into his organization in 1994 for *Charisma* magazine and was disturbed by his apparent wealth and that his ministry would not release budget figures and, at the time, was not filling out the 990 tax forms that the government demands of all nonprofits. I was even more disturbed when I interviewed him, because his aides fell into helpless laughter—and onto the floor—every few minutes. Then when I saw him at a prayer meeting trying to get everyone to laugh in the Spirit, I got so disgusted, I wrote an exposé for Hank Hanegraaf's Christian Research Institute.

By then the renewal had been tamed considerably. Many of the charismatic churches had retrenched and done away with freewheeling services that lasted up to three hours. They cut worship time to less than ninety minutes, to make services more seeker-friendly. Others quietly stopped teaching about spiritual renewal and instead had their people read and study the popular bestseller *Forty Days of Purpose* by Rick Warren or Henry Blackaby's *Experiencing God*, which, despite its title, had nothing to do with charismatic gifts. Still others shelved the idea of praying for spiritual gifts and invested in "spiritual gifts inventories" for their congregations—workbooks that help a person determine his or her spiritual gifts, sometimes using lists of items to be checked off. However, these inventories mixed the supernatural gifts, such as prophecy and discernment of evil spirits, with abilities, such as hospitality or giving, watering down the whole concept of a supernatural gifting of the sort the apostle Paul discussed in his letters to Timothy.

There were rare exceptions. Rick Evans, pastor of the Cleveland Vineyard, in an article in *Cutting Edge*, said spiritual gifts must be nurtured and taught. "One of the things I did as we planted our church was to regularly teach about the Holy Spirit," he said. "I wanted our core group to be biblically thoughtful about who the Spirit is and I wanted God to birth genuine faith in our group that the power of God is for *today*."

So he brought up the topic, and soon:

> I saw the fruit of my labors—God began raising up a core of men and women who welcomed the power of God's Spirit into their lives. . . . Instead of reacting passively to sickness and other difficulties, a growing number of our folks began to pray with greater authority that God would heal or break into problematic areas. In time, we started seeing healing after healing. Real faith started being born in our hearts.

Instead of reading a spiritual gifts inventory, his leaders laid hands on each other "to receive a spiritual gift of God's choosing," he said. They did it at renewal meetings, retreats, conferences—it was something natural and frequent.

But most churches did nothing like this, and once powerful churches became very ordinary.

Some people hoped that the aftermath of September 11 might bring radical change. Traumatized Americans streamed into the nation's churches on Sunday, September 16—and streamed right back out again within a few weeks when they heard nothing new from the pulpit.

"The sad outcome is that when we needed great leadership, we didn't have any guts," pollster George Barna told *Christianity Today* in 2002. "That moment of opportunity was squandered."

Things have gotten so boring that former *LA Times* religion writer John Dart, in a 2006 piece for the *Christian Century*, referred to the "rise, fall and diffusion" of the charismatic movement and its "domestication" into being an "arguably inconsequential" revival. In 1976 Anglican Bishop Michael Marshall predicted the Episcopal Church would be either "charismatic or dead" within ten years. Today it is neither, but its charismatic core has fled.

In the spring of 2007 I contacted David Anderson, an Episcopal priest, whose American Anglican Council had served as a rallying point for many charismatics. What, I asked him, had happened to the once powerful renewal?

"It's more relevant than it's ever been," he told me, "because the leadership on the firing line are products of the charismatic renewal. Without it, we wouldn't have had these people. Right now we need to survive the war we are in; we're forming soldiers for the battle that is now."

He referred to the outstanding lawsuits that some dioceses have thrown against Episcopal leaders who have bolted the denomination. "I believe the entire charismatic teaching will come back," he added, "but right now people are involved in legal strategies and defense; the energy is going into the battle now."

So not only is the energy not there to bring a new generation into the movement, but, as Anderson said, the renewal is irrelevant to current realities. Instead of spiritual power, they need a good legal defense!

The Spirit Overseas

A lot of the world is not at this low point. During two trips to India, one in 1994 and one in 2006, I met with church leaders who told me the one form of Christianity that's growing there is Pentecostalism. I found the same thing during a 1997 trip to Iceland. Some of the "Toronto blessing" leaders had conducted missions across the North Atlantic, setting a few fires in Iceland. The religious leaders I interviewed there all informed me that the Pentecostals and charismatic Lutherans were the only ones making a dent in the overwhelming secularity of that island.

At least one-quarter of the world's two billion Christians are Pentecostal or charismatic, according to the World Christian Database. In 2006 the Pew Forum on Religion and Public Life released an enormous study of the demographics, beliefs, and practices of Pentecostals and charismatics in ten countries. In the United States, Chile, Kenya, and South Africa, one in five people are Pentecostal or charismatic; in fact this is 23 percent of the American population. Even larger concentrations are in Brazil (34 percent of the general population); Guatemala and the Philippines, both at 40 percent.

The survey pointed out that supernatural activity, such as healing, speaking in tongues, and prophecy, is common in the church services of these people. Large majorities of those surveyed reported seeing divine healing; people in eight out of ten of the countries (India and South Korea being the exceptions) said they have received direct revelations from God; and majorities of those polled in seven of the countries said they had either personally experienced or seen an exorcism. India, South Korea, and the United States were the exceptions there.

The poll showed what is already generally known: Pentecostals and charismatics outdo all other Christian groups in church attendance, literal views of Scripture, evangelizing unbelievers, and other accomplishments. It's curious, though, that even when many people attend services replete with spiritual gifts, only a minority of Pentecostals and charismatics in six countries regularly pray in tongues. Only in South Korea, the United States, and the Christianized regions of India is that percentage close to half of all renewed Christians. Only in Guatemala do more than half of the Christians employ that spiritual gift.

In May 2007 editor Lee Grady wrote a column on *Charisma*'s website, urging readers not to be ashamed of Pentecostal gifts. "Some modern charismatics and Pentecostals who prefer seeker-friendly worship and user-friendly sermons have stopped offering prayer for the baptism in the Holy Spirit at their altars," he wrote. "They don't want to offend the crowd by encouraging anything too weird or embarrassing. They prefer church to be neat, orderly, and rational. They want a faith that can be controlled."

David Frederickson writes in his book *When the Church Leaves the Building* of the way the Spirit has been utterly quenched and the typical church looks nothing like the model Paul suggested in 1 Corinthians 14:26–31.

> One would be hard pressed to find even one of the elements [Paul] describes present in the Sunday morning meeting typical of most church gatherings today. [Instead] leaders have carefully planned an event to move from one predetermined segment to another while anticipating potential distractions with a planned response.

Thus the mature Christians, who may be getting nudges from the Holy Spirit, are outfoxed by a controlling pastor. If they want to offer a psalm, hymn, song, prophecy, tongue, or whatever else is included in the 1 Corinthians 14 passage, their ability to share it is cut off by their pastor, who controls access to the microphone.

"Pastors don't want to be bothered by interruptions or challenges to their power," Pentecostal historian Vinson Synan told me. "You never know. Some prophet may, like Nathan to King David, say, 'Thou art the man!'"

The current downturn, he added, "is all part of the ebb and flow of revivals. The freshness wears off and people return to the routine. In my own local church, it's hard to go. The pastor rattles on and on, there's no congregational participation, and everything comes from the pulpit. If the pastor has lost his fresh spirituality, he goes back to being in control."

Not a Distraction

Considering the messiness of spiritual gifts, "It's no wonder that so many Pentecostal pastors have quietly dismissed the role of prophecy in their churches," wrote Sacramento pastor Scott Hagan in *Ministries Today* back in 2005. Because of the "shallow goofiness" of those who prophesy, "some [ministers] have become so discouraged by this cycle that shepherding the gifts becomes a process of damage control and not much else," he said.

A charismatic church is "God's clear design for this age," he added, and the gifts "were never intended to be a distraction or a burden to the church." But they are treated as such.

I looked about for someone who actually uses these troublesome spiritual gifts in a winsome fashion. Canadian evangelist Patricia King runs an "extreme prophetic" ministry, whereby she and a team of evangelists take supernatural encounters with God to the streets. Basically this is personal prayer for people, accompanied by any prophetic insights team members might have.

"People are not hungry for institutionalized religion; they are hungry for true encounters with God," King said in a 2004 interview published in *Charisma*. The article went on to say how people lined up outside a juice café in Kelowna, British Columbia, waiting for up to an hour to hear what the evangelists had to say to them. Some received personal words of encouragement; others became believers.

Christians are in such a reaction mode against any spiritual weirdness that they spurn any experience of God, an attitude King gently ridiculed in a February 2007 *Charisma* article. Supernatural encounters are a normal part of a believer's life, she said, yet today's evangelicals avoid them like the plague, saying they do not want to worship experience over God. She likens today's Christians to a bride approaching a groom at the altar, only to say:

> I vow to be your wife, to be faithful to you, to submit to you. . . . Don't expect to *experience* my love. I'm not into experience. I don't want our marriage to be based on experience. Oh, and I won't expect to feel your love, either. I will simply believe that you love me. I will stand faithfully on the words of this covenant every day, but I will not expect, nor will I pursue, experience in our relationship.

This, King added, is ludicrous. "Experience has everything to do with relationship," she explains. "It is impossible to enjoy a rich, passionate and meaningful relationship without experience."

Burned Out

It's understandable that some people run the other way at the thought of a charismatically tinged revival. The last one of any note began in 1995 in Pensacola, Florida, at the Brownsville Assembly of God. By the time I got there in 1997 to report on it, lines of people waited all day in the hot Florida sun to get in. The worship, the preaching, and the prayers afterward were electric. Steve Hill, the in-house revivalist, never seemed to run out of great sermons. He and John Kilpatrick, the pastor, worked together well. The worship was just right. The church even had a staff person designated to work with media people, a welcome change from some other revivals I had covered where churches were extremely antagonistic toward reporters. I got to interview both men the night I was there.

I never got back to Pensacola, but it wasn't long before I began hearing of dissension in the ranks. In time Hill departed for a church in Dallas, which cut the heart out of the revival. Kilpatrick also moved on, and by 2006 the church had shrunk from thousands of visitors to five hundred people on a Sunday morning. They were also stuck with a huge bill for all the new construction they put up to accommodate extra ministries.

"One former staff member told me that a large group of Brownsville members now attend a local Southern Baptist church in the city, while many others don't go anywhere," Lee Grady wrote in another column. The staff member told him that people had been leaving for several years and that he did not know "anyone who has not been hurt."

Grady, who had a spiritual experience himself while covering the revival, reminded readers that Korean pastor David Yonggi Cho had announced from Brownsville's pulpit that its revival would last until the second coming. So much for that prophecy.

"For those in Pensacola who were swept up in the ecstasy of those early years and then endured splits, resignations, debts and disappointments, the word 'revival' now has a hollow ring to it," Grady wrote.

Yet, when anyone tries to write the obituary on charismatics, the body keeps popping out of the grave. In the spring of 2007 Lifeway put out a survey showing that half of the 405 Southern Baptist pastors polled believe the Holy

Spirit bestows a "private prayer language" on believers today. (Forty-three percent disagreed and 7 percent didn't know.) This was surprising, considering that in November 2005 the denomination's foreign mission board announced it would not hire missionaries who prayed privately in tongues. Many Baptists agree the gift was in use two thousand years ago, but they say that what passes today for tongues and interpretation isn't the same thing as was current during New Testament times.

Ed Stetzer, Lifeway's research director, called the results of the poll "surprising." He said, "As a whole, Southern Baptists are less affirming of a private prayer language, so the fact that 50 percent of the pastors answered 'yes' is very surprising. There are a lot of implications birthed out of that. Southern Baptists have become—at least half of them—more open to a practice that was not mainstream one hundred years ago."

I contacted R. T. Kendall, the famous pastor of Westminster Chapel in London who's now retired in Florida. He functions as an unofficial evangelical-Calvinist theologian of the charismatic renewal. He experienced speaking in tongues decades ago but said little about the experience until recently.

"Southern Baptists," he sighed, "are generally the most anticharismatic people in the world." Of course charismatics have done their share to merit that disapproval, he added. "I am sympathetic with many of these people," he said of his charismatic brethren, "but also highly critical of them. Most charismatics are Arminian and have a minimal concept of the sovereignty of God. They tend to think that if we do this, God will do that. So they think they can manipulate him."

He also said charismatics are not strong on the essentials. "They like prophecy, teaching on blessings, and miracles," he said. "Then they get thin on the ground and people get disillusioned when they go to church and get nothing. We need to get back to the Bible, good expository preaching, and the basics of the faith. How many sermons in a given year are preached on the cross? On the blood of Jesus? There is an absence of interest in God for his own sake. Until the church rediscovers these truths, the honor of God's name will not be restored and we will be anemic."

Concerning his fellow Reformed theologians, he confided, "They are scared to death of tongues. They don't want anything that is not of God. I want to say to them lovingly that tongues is the only gift of the Spirit that challenges your pride. They want to be knocked down by the Spirit before they speak in tongues, and that rarely happens."

Graham Cooke, an author who is part of a team of pastors at The Mission, a church in Vacaville, California, in 2007 wrote *Prophecy and Responsibility*, a primer on how to regulate the gift of prophecy. His argument was that this is a valid gift and, if pastored rightly, can yield huge benefits.

"The more of this kind of prophecy we can have in church, the less we will need intensive, time-consuming pastoral care," he wrote. "People will actually be touched by God and come into the things of the Spirit themselves."

The problem is nervous, controlling leaders, who do not let the third person of the Trinity work, he explained. "Often the prophetic person may have done everything right," he said, "but the insecurity and inadequacy of the leadership can kill any response to the word."

This is the reason that the sheer openness to God that the folks in little Lisakovsk showed on that snowy day was so endearing. They hadn't learned yet how to say no.

10

◇◇◇◇◇◇◇◇◇◇

BRINGING THEM BACK

If They Want to Come

As I wrap up this manuscript, I'm aware that criticizing church has become quite the fashion. In early October 2007 John Eldredge, founder of Ransomed Heart Ministries in Colorado Springs and author of several bestsellers on Christian masculinity, did several short interviews for Beliefnet .com, including "Why I Took a Year Off Church."

> I don't think we've come to appreciate how utterly numbing most church experience is. Most people's church experience amounts to about an hour a week. It's the Sunday service. They are passive participants for the most part. They listen to a message, they hear some songs, some music, all in an attempt to sort of inspire and encourage. It is mind-numbing, most of it.
>
> So yes, I took a year off of church. Just because I was so sick of pretending. I was faking it; that was the problem. I was faking a holiness I didn't have, I was faking an enthusiasm that frankly wasn't there, and I said, "I can't do that. It's dishonest."

◇◇◇◇◇◇◇◇◇◇

It's good to take time off church, he added, "to find the real thing." He suggested reading the Scriptures and "connecting with people who love God." His year of studying the Psalms, he insisted, actually brought him closer to God.

I contacted Eldredge, and he told me he and his family had actually left the established church a decade ago and never looked back. He knows "hundreds" of people who have left church as well.

"It was not enriching their experience of God," he said. "People have very little margin now. All our lives are extraordinarily busy. Our tolerance level is diminished somewhat and we cannot bring ourselves to go through the motions anymore. You also don't have the free time to waste time, unless it's something you really want to do."

Church does meet the needs of newer Christians, he added, but for the most part, "They are not bringing people into a genuine encounter with God. Their core business is to bring forth a genuine encounter with God. If they do not get that done, they are failing at the basic level."

He, his wife, and their three sons now go to a house church in Colorado Springs. When he mentions his disenchantment with church while on speaking engagements, "There is this almost massive wholesale understanding," he said. "This is an epidemic. It is only going to grow. The accusation is that we're backsliding, but the fact is, we are living a richer Christian experience than ever. It's mature Christians who have opted out of church."

Disenchantment

I remembered I had read in an interview that John Whitehead, founder of the Rutherford Institute in Charlottesville, Virginia, had also given up on church and was having devotions at home with his wife and five children. White-head's conservative legal foundation was known for its numerous high-profile cases, including that of Paula Jones in her 1997 sexual harassment suit against President Clinton. When I called him, he said yes, he had left his church when it kicked out its pastor.

"He was not a glad-hander; he didn't go out in the community," Whitehead said. "The night they ousted him, they lined up people to talk against him. It was one of the dirtiest, nastiest things I had ever seen. I felt so sorry for him."

Whitehead and his family began studying the Bible and worshiping at home.

"I'd seen so much hypocrisy in the church, and we had so much of a better spiritual experience in the home," he said. "I got something out of church meetings in the 1970s, but by the 1990s it was the same formal thing.

"I have represented some of the biggest names in Christianity, and I have seen some of the contradictions in their lives. I got so disenchanted with the Dobsons, the Falwells, and the Robertsons, and I've rolled with the big names and I've seen their fund-raising tactics. We're supposed to turn the other cheek when people spitefully use us, but some of those guys don't even try to obey that."

He did express admiration for the late Francis Schaeffer, with whom he worked in the 1980s and who greatly influenced the founding of the Rutherford Institute. "He was the real deal," Whitehead said. "He expressed the same thing to me: he didn't go to church. It was not intellectually stimulating for him—or for me; I have studied the Bible a lot and I don't need someone to tell me about John 3:16 again."

He added, "I am running into a lot of young Christians who do not want to go to church. They may go occasionally, but they do not get much out of it. They do not trust authority. They are getting their spiritual experiences off the Internet. Then again, my oldest son went to a black church and came back saying what a great spiritual experience it was, the way they worshiped. And the sermon was short and to the point."

Serving the Dissatisfied

By the fall of 2007 I'd become aware of an intriguing new survey done by Willow Creek Church in South Barrington, Illinois. It was on the effectiveness of the local church. They interviewed fifteen thousand people on how they felt they were growing as Christians and got some surprising results. The typical church, they discovered, made a huge difference in people's lives early in their Christian walk, but the longer they were Christians, the less impact the church had.

In other words, the older the Christian, the more dissatisfied he or she was with the church. The researchers identified two segments of unhappy Christians: the "stalled" and the "dissatisfied." The former had been Christians for some time but were spinning their wheels spiritually. The latter group were mature Christians who felt church was *keeping* them from growing. Together these groups formed 25 percent of the responses—the "stalled" were 15 percent, and the "dissatisfied" were 10 percent. Many of these people were considering leaving, Willow Creek leaders said.

"We made a mistake," senior pastor Bill Hybels said at a church summit in the summer of 2007. "What we should have done when people crossed the line of faith and became Christians, we should have started telling people and teaching people that they have to take responsibility to become 'self-feeders.' We should have gotten people, taught them how to read their Bible between services, how to do the spiritual practices much more aggressively on their own."

I wondered if the problem were not so much people learning how to nourish themselves spiritually as it was the church serving up only baby food. I asked two of the Willow Creek researchers, Cally Parkinson and Terry Schweizer, about these conclusions. Schweizer said 95 percent of all respondents admitted to having been stalled at some point in their Christian walk, often due to painful circumstances that had thrown them for a loop.

"The 'stalled' are people who are early in their spiritual journey," Parkinson said. "They have not rooted their own relationship with Christ, so when something happens, they don't have a deep enough relationship to keep them from being stuck. A number have addictions and they acknowledge that. They have other issues they are wrestling with.

"The higher end of the journey where the 'dissatisfied' are, the idea is to reactivate their faith by getting them to serve in the church or do some evangelism. Those are catalytic experiences for people."

I remarked that I had interviewed many "dissatisfied" people and knew how unlikely it was that simply reinvolving themselves in church would get them back into the fold.

"If we could serve these people better, the dissatisfaction level would go down," Parkinson said. "These people are sold out to Jesus Christ, they tithe, they serve, they even bring people to their church, but the church doesn't resonate with them. It's only one part of their spiritual life."

Our conversation did not supply any solutions to this problem, and Schweizer remarked that there's always an undercurrent of discontentment in any church. Pastors they talked with, he said, were not surprised at the one in four ratio. Because the research is so new, it was impossible for the Willow Creek staff to know how much of a trend this is. They did not have several decades' worth of data behind them that would show whether the discontented were a new factor or a permanent fixture in the church.

About when do people start feeling unhappy about their church? "Innovation 2007," Leadership Network's publication, dealt with older Christians whose talents weren't being used in church.

"People on the sidelines become bored," wrote Robert Lewis, pastor of Fellowship Bible Church in Little Rock, Arkansas. He went on to say that bored parishioners are the most committed church members who had been pioneers. Their satisfaction level had gone up for five years, then plateaued and then began dropping in the seventh year. Such people have been controlled to death, he concluded.

"Today's church is feeling a desire to change the world," he added. "Yet too often, we pastors ask congregation members only to put the trimmings on *our* ministry. Too many pastors like me have wrongly bought into the 'catch and keep' mentality. The result is we wear out our staff and even worse, we lose our best people."

To keep such people, you have to release them into ministry, Lewis said. If you do not, they will leave anyway for an organization outside your church. Churches, he added, should be "equipping, networking, resourcing, launching, supporting and cheering when its best 'fish' go out and change the world."

At the end of 2006 Lifeway did a survey on church "switchers," people who had changed congregations instead of dropping out. Some 415 people were polled.

"The two very top reasons people switch is the church was not helping them develop spiritually—that was 28 percent— or they did not feel engaged or involved in meaningful work in the church. The latter was 20 percent," Scott McConnell, the associate research director, told me. "In one sense, it is a condemnation of the church, but it's also encouraging that people are hungry. They want more. They have not given up on God."

"How does one get the disenchanted back into church?" I asked.

"When we asked the formerly churched what would get them back, they said the number one thing was an invite from a friend or family member," he answered. "The friendliness and welcoming aspect is crucial."

Five Years On

I was so intrigued with Alan Jamieson's *A Churchless Faith* that when I heard he had written a sequel, I contacted him in Wellington, New Zealand, to ask about it. Sure enough, he had written *Church Leavers: Faith Journeys Five Years On* about his research with people who had left church but not reconnected five years later.

Instead of missing their past church life, he told me, these people's concerns about their former congregations had intensified during the five-year gap. A reviewer at Victoria University in Wellington called the second book "disquieting," because the book "underscores once again just how irrelevant or unhelpful the institutional church has become for so many reflective and intelligent believers today."

Jamieson told me his formerly churched subjects "are not rushing back into the charismatic, evangelical type of churches," he said, "because they feel nothing has changed there. They want something that broadens and deepens them."

Of New Zealand's four million inhabitants, 15–20 percent are involved in a church, he said. Another 30–40 percent of the country's population used to be involved in church, a huge spiritual brain drain.

"When you ask people as to why they've left, they're saying it's leadership struggles and lack of pastoral care," he said. "When you drill a little further, they say, 'My faith is undergoing a huge transformation and I have questions that were never addressed.' With charismatics here in New Zealand, if something goes wrong or you've lost a job or there's sickness, you're told, 'You need to learn to pray better' or 'Something is wrong with you.'"

As for him, he was moving on to a new ministry in Christchurch on New Zealand's south island. His newest project is called *Chrysalis*, a book on how to work through faith crises.

As for Me and My House

Whatever happened to the churchless situation that my brothers and I found ourselves in when I began this book? My oldest brother, Rob, found a Christian and Missionary Alliance church near his Seattle area home, thanks to his oldest daughter, who had heard about it from her schoolmates. He is very happy there, partly thanks to a pastor who keeps in touch and prays fervently for him.

My other brother, Steve, is part of the organizing committee for Young Life at a nearby high school. Young Life is how he and I both became believers back in the 1970s, and Steve says he wishes he could find a church that promoted Christianity and the gospel as powerfully as Young Life does. Until he does, his Sunday mornings will consist of a leisurely breakfast and the *New York Times*.

I am somewhere between the two. Shortly after I came back from Kazakhstan, I began attending church again because I wanted my daughter to attend Sunday school. I also wanted ninety uninterrupted minutes when I could think about God and worship. I was finding it impossible to get much in the way of personal Bible study done sandwiched between my full-time job and life at home with a two-year-old. Unfortunately, there's nothing at this church in terms of Bible studies or support groups for working moms at a convenient time. For now, the Sunday service will have to suffice.

And even that is really not enough, and none of my deeper questions ever get addressed. "Church is immature," said Eldredge in our interview, "and the overall experience doesn't nourish someone who is fairly mature. People do it for their kids, but as soon as the kids are gone, they are out of there because it wasn't meeting their needs."

Briefly I checked into my former church, but little had changed since I had left. The onus was on us who had left, until a well-known member of the community walked out. This shook up the leadership, but as far as I know, no meaningful changes ever took place there. Had I not left, though, I would have never experienced the twilight zone of nonbelonging that many Christians experience when they leave their churches. I used to look down on such people, until I became one of them. After doing this research, I found the leave-takers to be blameless with very few exceptions. They were the early ones; now there is a larger shaking up going on.

What is the answer? For many, it's house churches, as a lot of people have found them to be the answer to many problems that have been brought up in these pages. There's nothing like attending a group where you are missed if you are gone, where people know enough about you to intercede intelligently, and where your participation means something. I attended such a group years ago in Oregon and loved it. But in many areas of the country, including where I live now on the East Coast, there aren't enough house churches to constitute a meaningful alternative.

Which brings us back to local churches, many of which are not about to change. They would prefer to die first, and many will slowly fade into the sunset. Everything in such churches depends on the pastor, who must want to reach the more mature Christian and be willing to make the necessary changes to attract this group. I've not seen many churches like this, that concentrate on discipleship and leave the bottle-feeding to the megachurches, but I'm willing to bet such a church would do well in this era of dumbed-down, purpose-driven, seeker-friendly Christianity. But the pastor must be willing to tackle the hard questions or this experiment will fail. Just as I was tying up loose ends on this book, I attended a service where one of the preachers delivered a sermon on God's sovereignty along with the assurance that all things work to the best for those who love God. Just days before, the local papers were filled with the horrifying story of a believing Christian woman whose insane husband just drowned their three children in a hotel bathtub. It was all over the news. I sat in this service, wondering how this preacher could be so clueless with hundreds of well-read evangelical listeners sitting there. Most of them may have, like me, been wondering where was God's sovereignty in the midst of these horrific murders. A brilliant pastor would have mentioned the incident and tackled that in terms of his topic. That is the kind of creativity that will be needed to bring back the formerly churched.

I am not as concerned about the younger breed of churches that cater to the under-thirty-fives. They are reaching a

valuable subset of society, and most of the energy and creativity in American evangelicalism is geared toward that
group. But the bulk of the country's churched population is
over thirty-five, and those are the ones who are bailing out.
They don't get a whole lot out of churches in movie theaters,
coffeehouses, and the like, and simply telling them to become
"self-feeders" is begging the question of how broken the
system really is. Assume that most people are struggling and
not a few have broken hearts. Preach with that in mind.

Finally, I have seen what a great church should and could
be. Many of these discoveries came when I was doing research on covenant Christian communities in Houston, Evanston, Illinois, Ann Arbor, and other places. In their best
moments, they were like Camelot—a vision of beauty that
truly worked. Everyone lived within one to two miles of
the church, which created great possibilities in transforming a neighborhood. One could walk to many members'
homes. There was a "vision of the house" that demanded
a lot of commitment, which people were glad to give because they got a lot back. There was an introductory rite
by which you were introduced into the core beliefs of these
churches. Their gathered worship was intimate and passionate, mainly because people knew each other so well that
they were vulnerable with each other. There were physical
and emotional healings. People shared and gave away their
possessions. They helped with each other's children. They
were led by a group of elders, not by one pastor, which gave
these churches a balanced meal.

Instead of being insular, these communities were quite
attractive to the outsider and the unconverted. Visitors as a
custom were invited to people's homes on Sundays after the
service. As a college student in Portland, Oregon, I was invited to an elder's home one Sunday after visiting his church

in nearby Lake Oswego. The encounter changed my life, and I became best friends with that elder and his wife, plus joined their church. The covenant community movement of the 1970s had its problems, but it did a lot of things right, and there has not been anything in effectiveness and spiritual power like them in more than thirty years. And when the Shane Claibornes of this world do try to repeat this experiment, the world comes running to watch.

Right now, Christians all over the English-speaking world are casting about, looking for a solution to the present malaise. Like the builders on Nehemiah's wall, they have often operated too separately and too far apart. Their best efforts get diminished, then absorbed by the culture. Miracles happened in Acts 2 when Christians decided to share things in common, be willing to suffer together, and be part of a supernatural church. They can happen again if enough believers are willing to pay the price. Then people will begin craving church instead of quitting church and the exodus will be no more.

SOURCES

Chapter 1 The Flood Outward

11 *Religious attendance fell.* National Opinion Research Center, University of Chicago, General Social Survey, 2002.

11 *Two 2005 studies.* C. Kirk Hadaway and Penny Long Marler, "How Many Americans Attend Worship Each Week? An Alternative Approach to Measurement," *Journal for the Scientific Study of Religion* 44, no. 3 (September 2005): 307–22.

12 *A significantly smaller.* Bob Smietana, "Statistical Illusion," *Christianity Today* (April 2006): 86.

12 *The three fastest-growing.* 2007 *Yearbook of American and Canadian Churches,* see www.nccusa.org/news/080215yearbook1.html.

13 *Because the U.S.* "Number of Unchurched Adults Has Nearly Doubled Since 1991," posted on May 4, 2004, at www.Barna.org.

13 *The fraction.* City University of New York, "American Religious Identification Survey" (2001), see www.gc.cuny.edu/faculty/research-briefs/aris/key-findings.htm.

13 *Ten percent.* Mark Chavez, "The National Congregations Study: Background, Methods and Selected Results," University of Arizona National Congregation Study 1998, *Journal for the Scientific Study of Religion* 38, no. 4 (1999): 458–76.

14 *A Field Guide.* Cynthia Woolever and Deborah Bruce, *A Field Guide to U.S. Congregations* (Louisville, KY: Westminster John Knox, 2002).

19 *Then I found.* Andrew Strom, "The 'Out-of-Church' Christians," posted April 4, 2003, on the John Mark Ministries website: http://jmm.aaa.net.au/articles/12003.htm. Strom's book by the same title, written in 2004, can be found at http://www.revivalschool.com.

21 *And in the January.* Becky Pamer, "How to Survive Church: Hope for Disillusioned Churchgoers," *Discipleship Journal* (January–February 2006):
75–80.

21 *In March.* Rita Healy and David Van Biema, "Why Home Churches Are
Filling Up: There's No Pulpit Like Home," *Time* (February 27, 2006).

21 *In 2002.* Tim Stafford, "The Third Coming of George Barna," *Christianity
Today* (August 5, 2002): 33–38.

Chapter 2 The Irrelevant Church

27 *During the summer.* William Lobdell, "Religion Beat Became a Test of
Faith," *Los Angeles Times*, July 21, 2007, A1.

28 *"I don't know the guy."* Rod Dreher, "Religion Reporter Loses His Faith,"
posted July 21, 2007, at www.beliefnet.com.

30 *although the 2007 Yearbook. 2007 Yearbook of American and Canadian
Churches.*

30 *A sobering.* Jerry Filteau, "U.S. Catholic Population Up, but Use of Sacraments Down," Catholic News Service, *National Catholic Register* (July
16–22, 2006): 2.

31 *The book explains.* Michael Lindsay, *Faith in the Halls of Power: How
Evangelicals Joined the American Elite* (New York: Oxford University
Press, 2007).

34 *In 2000 Lauren.* Lauren F. Winner, "Sex and the Single Evangelical," posted
January 2000, at www. beliefnet.com.

34 World *magazine ran.* Gene Edward Veith, "The Christian Cosmo Girl,"
World, February 19, 2000.

36 *"I think of Mark."* Stanton L. Jones, "The Loving Opposition: Speaking the
Truth in a Climate of Hate," *Christianity Today* (July 19, 1993): 19–25.

38 *When the* Wittenburg Door. Flip Barney, "Recovering a Christian View:
Interview with Stephen Mansfield," *Wittenburg Door* (July–August 2007):
12–17.

38 *"Much of what goes on."* Frederick Buechner, *Secrets in the Dark: A Life
in Sermons* (San Francisco: HarperSanFrancisco, 2006).

39 *The people who are.* Arthur S. Farnsley, "Flea Market Believers," *Christianity Today* (October 2006): 114–21.

39 *Farnsley surfaced.* Cathy Grossman, "Faith Found outside Church," *USA
Today*, January 9, 2008.

44 *"The world is thirsty."* Shane Claiborne, *The Irresistible Revolution* (Grand
Rapids: Zondervan, 2006).

46 *"These kinds of offers."* Bob Sorge, *Unrelenting Prayer* (Greenwood, MO:
Oasis House, 2005), 52.

Chapter 3 Searching for Community

50 *But the church.* George Barna, *Revolution* (Wheaton: Tyndale, 2005).

51 *It also got a riposte.* Kevin Miller, "No Church? No Problem," *Christianity
Today* (January 2006): 69–71.

51 *amid all of the bells.* Clint Rainey, "Mega Burnout," *Dallas Morning News,* July 25, 2005.

53 *Newer churches.* Jesse Noyes, "Bye-Bye First Baptist," posted December 21, 2007, at www.slate.com.

53 *Almost one in four.* Lynn Smith-Levin, Matthew Brashear, and Miller McPherson, "Social Isolation in America: Changes in Core Discussion Networks over Two Decades," *American Sociological Review* (June 2006): 353–75.

53 *"This new social detachment."* Clarence Page, "Socially Marooned?" *Washington Times,* July 6, 2006, A19.

54 *Sitting in a pew.* Stephanie Simon, "God's Call Comes by Cell Phone," *Los Angeles Times,* May 16, 2006.

55 *Here, no child.* Chris Weinkopf, "A Community of Faith," *American Enterprise* (May 2006): 33–36.

58 *According to a.* "House Churches Are More Satisfying to Attenders Than Are Conventional Churches," Barna Update (January 8, 2007), www.Barna .org.

61 *In January 2007.* "House Church Involvement Is Growing," Barna update (June 19, 2006), www.Barna.org.

Chapter 4 Emergence and Resurgence

71 *Mark Driscoll told.* Jason Bailey, "Men Are from Mars Hill," posted on July 4, 2006, at ChristianityToday.com.

71 *According to an.* David Kinnaman, "A New Generation of Adults Bends Moral and Sexual Rules to Their Liking," posted on October 31, 2006, at www.Barna.org.

74 *"The feeling of being."* David Kinnaman, "Bench Warmers," *Ministry Today* (May–June 2006): 18.

78 *famous evangelical leaders.* "Major Christian Leaders Are Widely Unknown, Even Among Christians," posted on November 27, 2006, at www .Barna.org.

Chapter 5 The Loneliest Number

85 *These are record levels.* Sam Roberts, "51% of Women Are Now Living without Spouse," *New York Times,* January 16, 2007, A1.

85 *Pew Research Center.* Pew Research Center, "Are We Happy Yet?" February 13, 2006, www.pewforum.org.

86 *In October 2005.* Brian Wilcox, "Religion, Family and the General Social Survey," *Religion and Ethics Newsweekly* (October 19, 2005).

87 *"I asked a singles pastor."* Ellen Varughese, *The Freedom to Marry* (Olathe, KS: Joy Press, 1992), 45.

89 *Churches teach.* Debbie Maken, *Getting Serious about Getting Married* (Wheaton: Crossway, 2006), 83.

93 *"Faith and Family."* John C. Green, "Faith and Family in America," *Religion and Ethics Newsweekly*, survey, October 21, 2005, www.pbs.org/wnet/religionandethicsweek908/interview.html.

94 *"It is cruel."* Alveda King, *I Don't Want Your Man, I Want My Own* (Chicago: Lushena Books, 2001).

95 *one from the singles.* "Peachtree Presbyterian Church Survey on Single Sexuality," January 1994.

95 *For their 1991 book.* Carolyn Koons and Michael Anthony, *Single Adult Passages: Uncharted Territories* (Grand Rapids: Baker, 1991).

95 *Alan Guttmacher Institute.* "Facts in American Teens' Sexual and Reproductive Health," September 2006, www.guttmacher.org/pubs/fb_ATSRH.html.

99 *getting a mate.* Rabbi Shmuley Boteach, *Dating Secrets of the Ten Commandments* (New York: Doubleday, 2000).

Chapter 6 Not So Solid Teaching

102 *In 1993 he found.* George Barna, *Today's Pastors* (Ventura, CA: Regal, 1993), 51–71.

102 *An updated 2006 poll.* George Barna, "Pastors Feel Confident in Ministry but Many Struggle in Their Interaction with Others," July 10, 2006, Barna.org.

102 *"Both clergy and laity."* Elizabeth Morgan, "Effective Preaching: An Ethical Obligation," *Christian Ethics Today* (February 2002).

107 *In the summer.* "Lifeway Research Surveys Formerly Churched: Can the Church Close the Back Door?" October 9, 2006, www.lifeway.com.

108 *"What's offered in church."* Charles Colson, "Soothing Ourselves to Death," *Christianity Today* (April 2006): 116.

110 *Both secular and Christian.* David Wilkerson, "That Dreadful Day No One Wants to Talk About," *World Challenge Pulpit Series*, February 5, 2007.

110 *In another newsletter.* David Wilkerson, "Whatever Happened to Repentance Preaching?" *World Challenge Pulpit Series*, January 15, 2007.

114 *In a September 1, 2007, post.* Sherman Haywood Cox II, "Can God Count on the Black Preachers—Where Are the Prophets?" posted September 1, 2007, at www.Soulpreaching.com.

Chapter 7 Is the Pastor the Problem?

120 *"On my worst nights."* Barbara Brown Taylor, *Leaving Church: A Memoir of Faith* (San Francisco: HarperSanFrancisco, 2006).

121 *In an essay.* Christine A. Scheller, "Sorrow but No Regrets: My Life in the Troubled, Redemptive Church," *Christianity Today* (July 2007): 40–41.

122 *Seventy-five percent.* John Fountain, "No Place for Me: I Still Love God, but I've Lost Faith in the Black Church," *Washington Post*, July 17, 2005, 31.

123 *These leaders.* Alan Jamieson, *A Churchless Faith* (London: SPCK Publishing, 2002).

124 *"As they leave."* Ibid.

124 *"Working hard."* Ibid.

125 *"Our culture says."* Jeff Bailey, "The Un-Busy Pastor: Redefining a Life Well-Lived," *Cutting Edge* (Spring 2002).

127 *"They have been."* Andy Butcher, "When Christians Quit Church," *Charisma* (February 2005): 35.

127 *In July 2006.* "Pastors Feel Confident in Ministry, but Many Struggle in Their Interaction with Others," posted July 10, 2006, at www.Barna.org.

128 *Barna says.* "Surveys Show Pastors Claim Congregants Are Deeply Committed to God but Congregants Deny It," posted January 10, 2006, at www.Barna.org.

128 *"Just having vision."* Rick Joyner, "Spiritual Authority: Understanding Leadership," *Morning Star* 1, no. 6 (1991).

130 *I learned this.* "Innovation 2007: Connecting Innovators to Multiply," Leadership Network (Dallas: Source Publications, 2007).

130 *Many pastors' conferences.* David Wilkerson, "Seeking the Face of God," *World Challenge Pulpit Series*, November 7, 2005.

131 *"Many ministers are alone."* Gary Wilkerson, "Why Pastors' Conferences?" *World Challenge Pulpit Series*, 2006.

132 *"Many denominations."* Joyner, "Spiritual Authority," 4.

Chapter 8 The Other Sex

135 *"The typical evangelical."* Scott Pinzon, *CBA Marketplace* (August 1999).

139 *According to George Barna's.* "Spirituality May Be Hot in America, but 76 Million Adults Never Attend Church," posted March 20, 2006, at www.Barna.org.

139 *"Today's overextended woman."* Dannah Gresh, *The Secret of the Lord: The Simple Key That Will Revive Your Spiritual Power* (Nashville: Thomas Nelson, 2005).

141 *She was soon called.* David Bayly, "Come Out from Behind Those Skirts: An Open Letter to Frank James," posted February 16, 2006, at www.Baylyblog.com.

141 *"We are certainly glad."* Jeff Robinson, "CBMW Expresses Concerns over Teaching of Carolyn Custis James. Part I: Women Leashed by Church's 'Blueprint'?" posted March 27, 2006, at www.gender-news.com.

144 *In its update.* Bob Smietana, "Looking for the Next Big Thing: A Christian Publishing Update," *Christianity Today* (June 2007): 44–47.

146 *The* Washington Post. Amy Joyce and Frank Swoboda, "9–5 Gives Way to 24-7," *Washington Post*, March 10, 2000, E1.

147 *"One of the things."* Jeff Bailey, "The Un-Busy Pastor: Redefining a Life Well-Lived," *Cutting Edge* (Spring 2002): 15.

147 *The classes are for women.* Rose French, "Baptist Seminary to Offer Homemaking for Women Only," the Associated Press, August 11, 2007.

Chapter 9 Bewildered Charismatics

159 *"One of the things."* Rick Evans, "Maintaining the Balance: The Power of the Holy Spirit and Church Planting," *Cutting Edge* (Fall 2003): 2–4.

159 *"The sad outcome."* Tim Stafford, "The Third Coming of George Barna," *Christianity Today* (August 5, 2002).

159 *Things have gotten.* John Dart, "Charismatic and Mainline," *Christian Century* (March 7, 2006).

161 *At least one-quarter.* "Spirit and Power: A Ten-Nation Survey of Pentecostals," Pew Forum on Religion and Public Life, October 5, 2006.

162 *In May 2007.* J. Lee Grady, "Pentecost Sunday: It's Nothing to Be Ashamed Of," posted May 25, 2007, at www.charismamag.com.

162 *"One would be."* David Frederickson, *When the Church Leaves the Building* (Family Room Media, 2006).

163 *"It's no wonder."* Scott Hagan, "Help! Someone Is Speaking in Tongues," *Ministries Today* (2005): 33–34.

163 *"People are not."* Julia Loren, "Canadian Evangelist Takes Prophetic Ministry to the Extreme," *Charisma* (November 2004): 26.

164 *Christians are in such.* Patricia King, "Living in the Throne Room," *Charisma* (February 2007).

165 *"One former staff."* J. Lee Grady, "Don't Drop the Ark," *Charisma* (July 2006): 6.

165 *In the spring of 2007.* Libby Lovelace, "Lifeway Research Studies the Use of Private Prayer Language," June 4, www.lifeway.com.

167 *"The more of this."* Graham Cooke, *Prophecy and Responsibility* (Vacaville, CA: Brilliant Book House, 2007).

Chapter 10 Bringing Them Back

169 *"I don't think."* Patton Dodd, "Why Men Don't Like Church," four interviews with John Eldredge, posted October 2007 at www.Beliefnet.com.

172 *By the fall.* "Spiritual Life Survey Results," Willow Creek Church (Summer 2007): 28–31.

172 *"We made a mistake."* www.revealnow.com/story.asp?storyid=49.

174 *About when.* "Innovation 2007: Connecting Innovators to Multiply," Leadership Network (Dallas: Source Publications, 2007).

174 *"Today's church."* Ibid.

174 *At the end of 2006.* "Study of Adults Who Switch Churches: Why They Flee," Lifeway Research (April 2007), www.lifeway.com.

175 *A reviewer at.* This quote is attributed to Chris Marshall, a senior lecturer at Victoria University in Wellington, New Zealand, in a May 17, 2006, post on the Prodigal Kiwis Blog, prodigal.typepad.com.